SEXUAL VIOLENCE

SEXUAL VIOLENCE

THE UNMENTIONABLE SIN

Marie M. Fortune

The Pilgrim Press
Cleveland, Ohio

The Pilgrim Press, Cleveland, Ohio 44115

Printed in the United States of America
The paper used in this publication is acid free and meets the minimum requirements of the American National Standard for Information Sciences-Permanence of Paper for Printed Library Materials, ANSI Z39.48-1984

96 95 94   10 9 8

Library of Congress Cataloging-in-Publication Data

Fortune, Marie M.
Sexual violence.

1. Sex crimes. 2. Sex offenders. 3. Violent crimes. 4. Rape.
5. Child molesting. I. Title.
HQ71.F67   1983   364.1'53   83-3948
ISBN 0-8298-0652-0 (pbk.)

FOR ANNE

WHO SUSTAINS MY SPIRIT,
AND EMPOWERS MY MINISTRY.

Contents

Acknowledgments

I thank with deepest gratitude the following people who made this book possible:

For their encouragement in the beginning, Nanette Roberts, William Sheek, Letha Scanzoni, Peggy Way, Lois Selmar, and Faith Johnson.

For their careful and caring review of many drafts, Lucy Forster-Smith, Elizabeth Stellas, Mark Dion, Amelie Ratliff, Maryviolet C. Burns, Anita Mendez, Doris Stevens, Margaret Farley, Beverly Wildung Harrison, and especially Anne L. Ganley.

For their patient typing of the manuscript, Marcia Macomber, Linda Jones, and Kathy Johnson.

For their contributions of additional material, Nancy Ousley and Denise Hormann.

For their careful editing and support, Esther Cohen and Pamela Nelson.

For his patient presence, Eos.

For their support and interest, Marie VanBronkhorst and Beverly and Don Knuth.

For their inspiration and courage, the unnamed women and men who have shared their stories of sexual violence with me.

FOREWORD

" . . . BUT NO ONE EVER COMES TO ME WITH THIS
PROBLEM . . . "

This is the most common response I hear from clergymen
whom I question about their pastoral contact with victims and
perpetrators of sexual violence. (I say clergymen because
women pastors are more frequently approached with this
problem.) The clergymen then draw disturbing conclusions
from this piece of information: "Because no one ever comes to
me with this problem, there is no problem among my congregation. Since there is no problem, I do not need to learn
about it." Seldom does it occur to a pastor that the reason he
does not hear about his congregation's experiences of sexual
violence is that he has made it clear that he is not prepared to
hear or is unable to be of assistance. *Ironically, we have not
heard about sexual violence in the Church because we have
not spoken about it.* The silence is not an indication of the
absence of the problem; it is itself a loud, orchestrated denial
of a problem which certainly exists. For centuries the message has been effectively communicated: speak not about
rape, incest, child molestation—especially in church. So the
sin of sexual violence (and some even argue it is no sin) has
remained unmentionable.

Why has the silence persisted? The long and painful history

of the patriarchal oppression of women has contributed to denial of sexual violence as a problem. The victims of sexual violence are primarily women and girl children. This victimization of women and girls has been lost in silence, regarded as insignificant. Not coincidentally, this silence has served to maintain the status quo of women's oppression and isolation.

Victims of sexual violence have tended to keep their experiences private, shared if at all only among closest friends. This is largely a consequence of the stigma society attaches to victims. Victims who have felt that they will be blamed for their victimization have hesitated to tell anyone about it. In addition, the response of many institutions, including the church, has reinforced the privatization of sexual violence. The minister who tries to counsel a victim and discourages her from reporting the incident, the doctor who treats the child victim of sexual abuse and tells no one else, the police officer who takes a superficial report but tells a victim that little can be done, and the prosecutor who refuses to file charges because the case is inadequate all serve to further privatize the victim's experience. This is especially the case when the victim knows the assailant—he is a friend or family member. Then she is encouraged and feels obligated to keep the secret, to keep it in the family, to keep silent.

The silence is perpetuated by shame and confusion. Sexual violence, in most people's minds, has something to do with sex and so is shameful for the victim. In both society and church we are confused about the nature of sexual violence and often do not recognize it for what it is. The distinction between sexual activity and sexual violence has become blurred. As a result, people minimize the abusive nature of coercive sex as well as sexual violence. Silence is the result.

Finally, the silence is reinforced by the lack of ethical and theological clarity about sexual violence especially as found in the religious community. A chronic misplacement of ethical concern in the area of sexuality has meant that the sin of sexual violence has not clearly been identified nor has the offender been held accountable. Justice has not been done. Once again the religious community has followed the lead of society and, floundering in confusion, has never taken up sexual violence as an ethical and theological issue. Thus it has not provided adequate guidance to its clergy and laypeople to enable them to deal with sexual violence. This persistent silence has led to painful consequences for many. Victims remain isolated in their suffering, pastors remain oblivious to their people's needs, society ignores the extent of the problem and responds only occasionally to the most severe situations, and the church continues to misplace its ethical concern and avoids the task before it.

Silence begets more silence, the tightness of the circle is overwhelming at times. The victim's silence about her or his experience feeds society's silence which encourages the victim's silence to continue. The pastor's silence reflects and sustains society's silence which insures the victim's silence. Will these circles be unbroken? Only so long as our collective desire is not to know the extent and severity of acts of sexual violence against women, children, and men. We have for too long denied the evidence which has appeared in the midst of the silence for fear that it was true. We have all participated in this conspiracy of silence. We do not want to know. Hearing and acknowledging the reality of sexual violence, tracing its roots, seeing its victims and its aftermath are disquieting, frightening, and at times overwhelming experiences. So we have collectively passed by on the other side, unwilling or unable even to see and hear the reality before us.

The silence is being broken. Since the early 1970s individual victims have bravely shared their experiences of rape, incestuous abuse, and molestation. The conspiracy has been revealed. Only at great cost to us as individuals, church, and society do we seal our ears to their voices. No excuse, no rationalization will do any longer. We are being called loudly and clearly to address the Unmentionable Sin—to bring healing and justice where there is brokenness and offense, to direct righteous anger at the abuse of the holiest of temples, the human being.

This book is part of breaking the silence in the church surrounding sexual violence. It does so in such a way as to enable the church to respond to its calling to no longer pass by on the other side.

The book is divided into two parts. Part 1, "An Ethical Perspective," begins the task of understanding our Christian tradition and its neglect of sexual violence as an ethical issue. The societal context and the confusion about sexual activity and sexual violence provides the backdrop for a critique of the theological and ethical tradition. From this critique the ethical question is restated, the categories of ethical discussion are redefined, and a new ethical framework for understanding and responding to sexual violence is put forth.

Building on this theological and ethical foundation, Part 2, "A Pastoral Perspective," develops an effective and compassionate pastoral response to victims and perpetrators of sexual violence. This response can and should be implemented by the whole church, clergy and lay. Finally, the responsibility of the church to address the causes of sexual violence is delineated and suggestions are made for ways to do this effectively.

I have come to write this book after five years of work with the Center for the Prevention of Sexual and Domestic Violence, which provides education and training within the church about sexual violence. In these five years, the church's sometimes stubborn silence has discouraged me; but the willingness of some segments of the faith community, particularly laypeople, to listen, speak, and act boldly, has empowered me and has reassured me that the silence is being broken. I brought to this writing task my experience as a woman, my analysis as a feminist, my faith as a Christian, and my learning as a pastor and educator. I pray that the result will be of value to the reader and will make it possible finally to name the Unmentionable Sin, and in this naming to act to eradicate sexual violence from our lives.

Sexual Violence

Part 1.

~~~~~~

An Ethical Perspective

~~~~~~

AT TIMES WE CONDEMN RAPE AS A MONSTROUS, CRIMINAL ACT; AT OTHERS, WE SLOUGH IT OFF AS A MILDLY DIRTY JOKE, TREATING IT AS NOTHING MORE SERIOUS THAN A MINOR SKIRMISH IN THE INEVITABLE "BATTLE OF THE SEXES." AS THE ARCHETYPAL, ANTISOCIAL CRIME, . . . RAPE CALLS FORTH OUR GREATEST MORAL OUTRAGE AND OUR GREATEST CRY FOR VENGENCE. BUT CO-EXISTING WITH THESE ATTITUDES ARE OTHERS, IN WHICH RAPE IS DISMISSED WITH A KNOWING WINK AS A NATURAL CONSEQUENCE OF THE SEXUAL GAME IN WHICH MAN PURSUES AND WOMAN IS PURSUED. WHAT IS CALLED "RAPE," THEN, IS THOUGHT TO BE ONLY AN UNSOPHISTICATED SEDUCTION; AT MOST IT IS A MINOR BREACH OF OUR SOCIAL STANDARDS.

Lorenne Clark and Debra Lewis,
Rape: The Price of Coercive Sexuality

There is bewilderment, embarrassment, and ambivalence in our society about the nature of sexual aggression and violence. But the real difficulty lies in this society's persistent confusion of sexual violence with sexual activity. For many, in both experience and attitudes, sexual activity and sexual violence have become equated; distinctions between the two are seriously blurred.

1

For example, a recent survey of teenagers between the ages of 14 and 18 revealed that it is acceptable for a boy to force sexual contact with a girl if she arouses him sexually or leads him on, if they have dated for a long time, or if she says she is willing to have sex but changes her mind. Fifty-four percent of the males surveyed agreed that forced sex was acceptable under these circumstances and forty-two percent of the females agreed.[1]

Susan Griffin describes an experience common for women: "My initiation to *sexuality* [emphasis added] was typical. Every woman has similar stories to tell—the first man who *attacked her* [emphasis added] may have been a neighbor, or family friend, an uncle, her doctor, or perhaps her own father."[2] The prevalence of such encounters leads women to accept forced sexual contact as normal; hence, the confusion between sexual activity and sexual violence.

Christian ethics and theology have provided little guidance in understanding the difference between sexual activity and sexual violence for a society faced daily with experiences that reflect the confusion between the two. Christian sexual ethics have often promoted the confusion of sexual activity with sexual violence. Furthermore, Christian ethics have failed to confront the problem of sexual violence itself; thus, there has been no mandate for Christians to address this widespread problem.

To respond adequately to the tragedies of rape and child sexual abuse and to develop and sustain both responsibility and fulfillment in our sexual activity, we must explore this confusion between sexual violence and sexual activity. In order to do this, we must first have a clear understanding of what sexual violence is. Then we will examine the nature and sources of the confusion between sexual violence and sexual activity and distinguish between the two phenomena. Finally, having drawn these new distinctions, we will discuss sexual violence as an ethical problem and posit a new set of Christian ethical principles to guide our activity. This discussion will provide the ethical and theological foundation for an effective and intentional response by the Christian community to the epidemic problem of sexual violence in our society.

Notes

1. Laurel Fingler, "Teenagers in Survey Condone Forced Sex," *Ms* Magazine (February, 1981), p. 23.
2. Susan Griffin, *Rape: The Power of Consciousness* (San Francisco: Harper & Row, 1979), p. 8.

Chapter 1

Definitions of Sexual Violence

Sexual violence is, first and foremost, an act of violence, hatred, and aggression. Whether it is viewed clinically or legally, objectively or subjectively, violence is the common denominator. Like other acts of violence (assault and battery, murder, nuclear war), there is a violation of and injury to victims. The injuries may be psychological or physical.[1] In acts of sexual violence, usually the injuries are both.

For many, the realization that sexual violence is primarily violent and only secondarily sexual in nature has been difficult to accept. There have been years of indoctrination that in "sex crimes" there are rapists who cannot control themselves and victims who really want to be raped. In this erroneous stereotype, sexual violence is seen as being primarily sexual in nature. In fact, rape and child sexual abuse are acts of violence which are injurious. Any victim of rape knows that she has experienced the most violent act possible short of murder. And any victim of child sexual abuse is haunted by the helplessness she felt at the hands of the molester who sought to control and exploit her.

Experience, which is the basis for all knowledge, has become the primary source of comprehending sexual violence. Those who have been raped have walked through "the valley of the shadow of death" and most have returned to tell about it. Whether or not physical violence was inflicted, the most common reaction of a victim is "I thought I was going to be killed." The victim is overwhelmed and overpowered by both

5

the physical strength and the hatred of the rapist. The fear
expressed by victims of child sexual abuse is similar.

> I had been asleep and woke up to find my father being
> sexual with me. I recall being in a state of terror, not
> quite knowing what was going on as I lay there for a few
> minutes and allowed him to touch me. . . . Mostly a
> feeling of growing up in an environment that was
> unsafe . . . I never felt my body was safe from violation.[2]

A response of fear would be expected from a child confronted
by physical force from a stranger. But even without overt
physical force and with someone known and trusted, the child
is overwhelmed, overpowered, and terrorized. In addition to
the terror that comes from the experience of coercion and
force, the child may experience the betrayal of a family relationship. These are the consequences of a violent act. It has
been largely through victims' telling of their experiences that
society has undergone a revolution in consciousness about
sexual violence since 1970. Finally, our society has begun to
comprehend that acts of sexual violence are violent, i.e., a
forced or coercive violation of another person. This understanding makes all the difference in the way we assist victims,
treat offenders, and go about trying to eliminate sexual violence altogether.

On the one hand, the sexual nature of sexual violence is
irrelevant. Violence is violence no matter what form it takes.
The body is assaulted, injury occurs, and there is the experience of physical and emotional pain. And yet the sexual aspect
of sexual violence is relevant. The nature of the assault makes
clear the totality of the violation of the person.[3] During the
attack or the abuse, the victim is not only out of control of
her/his situation, but the victim is also assaulted in the most
vulnerable dimension of the self. A sexual attack makes it
clear that something has been taken away. Power has been
taken away. The power to decide, to choose, to determine, to
consent or withhold consent in the most concrete bodily di-

mension, all vanish in the face of a rapist or child molester. Being forced sexually against one's will is the ultimate experience of powerlessness, short of death.

Sexual violence represents a profound violation of another person which is injurious and destructive. One definition of victim is "a living being sacrificed to some deity."[4] This definition of victim more than any other makes clear the consequence of violence. A living being, a person created in the image of God, is sacrificed to "some deity" everytime an adult is raped or a child molested. A person is made to become a victim, a living sacrifice, by an act of another person. One wonders if any deity could possibly be well-served by such an act.

Rape

Although legal definitions of rape vary from state to state, the most comprehensive definition refers to forced penetration by the penis or any object of the vagina, mouth, or anus against the will of the victim. Lesser forms of forced sexual contact are dealt with as assault and battery. This legal definition represents a significant improvement over previous rape laws which specified vaginal intercourse forced by a male on a female. These legal definitions describe what actually happens in rape situations and do not limit rape to penis-vagina intercourse. The current inclusive definition provides for oral or anal sex against the will of the victim. In addition, it does not specify the gender of the victim or offender as the previous laws did. Thus same-gender rape can be prosecuted as rape rather than under the old sodomy laws which made male rape of a male an illegal *sexual activity* rather than an assault. Theoretically a female could be an offender by using an object to penetrate a victim. The new laws place the emphasis on the assaultive aspect rather than on the sexual nature of the act.

Clinically, rape is regarded as a *pseudosexual act*. It is an act which has the appearance of sexual activity in that genital contact is involved. However, rape is only pseudosexual because it is committed in order to fulfill nonsexual needs related to power, anger, and aggression. Rape involves "hostility (anger) and control (power) more than passion."[5] Anger and a desire to dominate and control the victim are the primary motivations of the rapist. These factors are consistent with the victim's experience of sexual violence. The victim feels violated, dominated, and powerless.

Though society, offenders, and sometimes victims may view rape as sexual, rape is not a sexual experience. Rape is very different from consensual sexual activity. It is an act done to a victim, against her/his will. Even if the victim has an orgasm during the rape (as is sometimes the case), the experience is still not primarily a sexual one. This may be very disturbing for the victim: Both male and female victims who have had an orgasm during rape expressed guilt and confusion. They interpret the orgasm to mean that they *enjoyed* the experience, that the experience was sexual, and that they wanted it; otherwise, they reason, why would they have had an orgasm? In these situations, orgasm is a physiological response to fear combined with direct sexual stimulation. Sexual arousal to orgasm can be triggered by fear as well as by desire; the physiological response to both is similar.[6] This does not mean that the subjective experience for the victim is pleasurable. In many ways, this is yet another victimization: The victim is powerless to withhold even sexual response and feels betrayed by her or his own body. Still, the overriding experience of the rape victim is fear and violence.

For offenders as well, rape is not primarily a sexual experience. There is ample evidence that men who rape are not seeking sexual activity.

> It is commonly—and mistakenly—assumed that men who rape do so either because they are sexually aroused or because they are sexually frustrated, or both. In fact, as we have seen, the motives underlying such assaults

have more to do with issues of anger and power than with pleasure and desire. Rape is a pseudosexual act, a distortion of human sexuality, symptomatic of personality dysfunction in the offender, rather than a sexually satisfying experience.[7]

The majority of rapists report that they have one or more regular sexual partners. They are not seeking a sexual outlet *per se* and if they were, prostitutes are readily available.

Since rape is a pseudosexual act and is a symptom of conflict and anxiety, it would follow that rapists experience sexual dysfunction in their assaults more often than in consensual sexual activity. Nicholas Groth reports this to be the case.[8] Not only do rapists report dysfunction but also the absence of sexual satisfaction or pleasure from the assault.

> It is like animal sex, hard and rough, not gentle. There was no foreplay. I felt sick and disgusted about it after it was over. I knew this wasn't necessary. I was having sex regularly with three or four girls I knew at the time. I don't know why I did it.[9]

> After it was over, I felt a big letdown. It just wasn't worth it. The sex wasn't any good at all, and I didn't prove anything.[10]

Any pleasure that the rapist experienced came not from the sex but from other aspects of the assault.

> It was one of the most satisfying experiences I've ever had. I got more pleasure out of being aggressive, having power over her, her actions, her life. It gave me pleasure knowing there was nothing she could do . . . . My feelings were a mixture of sex and anger. I wanted pleasure, but I had to prove something, that I could dominate a woman . . . . The sex part wasn't very good at all.[11]

It is clear that both legally and clinically rape is an act of violence and aggression and is experienced as such by both the victim and the offender. The use of sexual organs does not make rape a sexual act. Rape uses sex as a weapon to do injury to another person. The fact that the sexual contact is inflicted against the will of the person and causes injury to that person makes rape a violent act.

Child Sexual Abuse

While rape usually represents a clearly assaultive situation, i.e., physically forced, child sexual abuse is more often coercive than assaultive. The offender—whether a stranger, someone known to the child, or a family member—takes advantage of the vulnerability of the child and coerces her/him into sexual activity. Therefore, the term "abuse" rather than "assault" is a more accurate designation. However, as in rape, child sexual abuse is a form of violence, for it results in both psychological and physical injury to its victim.

Legally, child sexual abuse is described using various terms. It may be considered rape if physical force is used and penetration takes place, or statutory rape if force is not used but the victim is underage and thus unable to give legal consent.[12] Sexual abuse without penetration (touching, fondling, masturbation, etc.) usually is defined as indecent liberties.

Clinically, child sexual abuse is the sexual exploitation of a child who is not developmentally capable of understanding or resisting the contact, and/or who is psychologically and socially dependent on the offender.[13] It may involve fondling, exhibitionism, masturbation, and genital penetration. The National Center for Child Abuse and Neglect also includes in the category of child sexual abuse commercial exploitation for prostitution or the use of children in the production of pornographic materials.[14]

There are two criteria which provide the parameters for understanding child sexual abuse as a form of violence and aggression. The first (as in rape) is the lack of consent on the part of the victim. However, in the case of child sexual abuse, the lack of consent is a given. Children, by definition, cannot give or withhold consent when approached sexually by an adult because they are immature, uninformed, and usually dependent on the adult. Consequently, they lack the real power to resist.[15] Therefore, any sexual contact between an adult and a child is abusive. The second criterion for understanding child sexual abuse has to do with whose self-interest is being served by the sexual contact and who is injured. Child sexual abuse describes "contacts or interactions between a child and an adult when the child is being used for sexual stimulation of that adult or another person."[16] The sexual *use* of a child disregards the child's welfare. The child becomes an object exclusively to meet the needs of the offender. The act is exploitative and, consequently, damaging to the child.

The sexual dimension of child sexual abuse contributes to confusion for the child victims.

> I remember the terror I felt and the confused feeling of being turned on [when my father touched me sexually] . . . Even now [as an adult], what I do recall about my father is that even though I was in a state of terror, it was also in a way very positive, since my father's sexual advances toward me were the only recalled demonstrated love that was expressed to me in my childhood.[17]

The child may experience positive physical feelings, affection, and a sense of self-worth simultaneously with terror and powerlessness. This combination, confusing to the child, encourages self-blame and discourages her/him from seeking help to stop the abuse.

Child sexual abuse presents a situation in which sexual activity is confused with sexual violence in the experience of both victim and offender and in the minds of the public. Lack of consent (by definition) and resultant injury to the victim are the basis on which to understand sexual contact between adult and child as abusive and violent.

Notes

1. Albert Bandura, *Aggression: A Social Learning Analysis* (Englewood Cliffs, N.J.: Prentice-Hall, Inc., 1973), p. 5.
2. Sandra Butler, *Conspiracy of Silence* (San Francisco: New Glide Publications, 1978), pp. 49-50.
3. Traditionally society's focus on the sexual nature of sexual assault has allowed society and the offender to avoid confronting the violence inherent in sexual assault. Now, however, we must be careful when focusing on the violence that we not begin to view sexual assault strictly as a physical attack. Rather we need to realize the sexual *and* the violent nature of the experience.
4. *Webster's New Collegiate Dictionary* (Springfield, Ma.: G.&C. Merriam Co., 1961), p. 950.
5. Nicholas Groth with Jean Birnbaum, *Men Who Rape* (New York: Plenum Press, 1979), p. 2.
6. Similarly, hyperventilation is a physiological response in which one takes shallow, short breaths. It may result from either sexual excitement or fear.
7. Groth with Birnbaum, p. 84.
8. "In our clinical work with identified rapists, we found that one out of every three offenders reported experiencing some sexual dysfunction during their offense, and we believe this to be a conservative estimate." Groth with Birnbaum, p. 84–85.
9. Quoted in Groth with Birnbaum, p. 94.
10. *Ibid.*, pp. 94–95.
11. *Ibid.*, p. 95.
12. "Underage" refers to boys and girls under 16 or 18 years old depending on state statutes. The more effective statutes indicate that underage persons are by definition unable to consent to sexual contact with an adult. See Chapter 4, "Consensual Sex and a New Sexual Ethic."
13. Mimeographed handout, "Sexual Abuse of Children," Sexual Assault Center, Harborview Medical Center, Seattle, Washington, May 1977.

14. U.S. Dept. of Health and Human Services, *Child Sexual Abuse: Incest, Assault, and Sexual Exploitation* (Washington, D.C.: U.S. Dept. of Health and Human Services, 1981), p. 1.
15. David Finklehor, "What's Wrong with Sex Between Adults and Children," *American Journal of Orthopsychiatry*, vol. 49 (October 1979), pp. 694–96.
16. U.S. Dept. of Health and Human Services, p. 1.
17. Sandra Butler, pp. 49–51.

Chapter 2

Confusing Sexual Activity and Sexual Violence

RAPE IS VIOLENCE, NOT SEX—A BUTTON SOLD BY
RAPE CRISIS CENTERS

. . . BUT LATELY I HAVE BEGUN TO WONDER ABOUT
THIS PERFERVID INSISTENCE THAT THE ACT [OF RAPE]
IS NOT SEXUAL IN NATURE, WHEN EVERY COUNSEL OF
COMMON SENSE SUGGESTS THAT IT IS, AT LEAST IN
PART. . . . [ONE] REASON FOR OUR RELUCTANCE TO
ACKNOWLEDGE THE TRUE CHARACTER OF RAPE [IS] THE
FACT THAT THE ATROCITY SAYS SOMETHING DISTURB-
ING ABOUT THE VERY NATURE OF SEXUALITY . . .

William Muehl, "Rape is a Sexual Act,"
Reflection

There are two extreme positions held on the nature of rape:
rape is violence or rape is sex. The force with which these two
positions are argued makes one pause and consider the meaning of this divergence of opinion.

When asked to define rape to a hypothetical stranger to this
culture, members of an adult church school class listed words
such as:

fear	sexual intercourse without consent
hurt	violence
violation	against your will
force	hostile

This list emphasizes the violence of rape, the lack of consent,

14

and the resulting fear and pain. Sexual terms are used only to describe the type of violence. This is an accurate description. While rape is sexual in nature, as the term "sexual violence" makes clear, the grammatical arrangement of the term is crucial. The noun is "violence," the basic dynamic of the experience. The adjective is "sexual," describing the type of violence. While the mechanics of rape are sexual, the primary motivation is not; it is violence.

Before 1970, the words used to describe rape would have been quite different. There would have been mostly sexual words describing a supposedly sexual act, e.g., clumsy seduction, sex that got out of hand, perversion, etc. Since 1970, our society has begun to look again at rape, to listen to the experiences of victims and offenders and, as a result, to redefine rape in more accurate terms. The emphasis placed by those in the anti-rape movement ("RAPE IS VIOLENCE, NOT SEX") represents an important corrective to previous beliefs and attitudes. The purpose of this emphasis is to undo the long-held belief that rape is primarily the sexual act of a man who cannot control his sexual feelings. The effort to redefine rape as primarily a violent act has succeeded so surprisingly well that the most common response to the question "What is rape?" now emphasizes its violent aggressive source. We have begun to distinguish between sexual violence and sexual activity.

But this is not all of the story. Perhaps we are now at a point where as a society we can begin to ask the more difficult question: What are the relationships between sexual violence, sexuality, and sexual activity? I suggest that this is first of all an analytical task drawing on the most current and accurate information we have from both victims and offenders and those who work with them. Second, this is an ethical task. What ethical norms can we posit which will guide not only our understanding of sexual violence as it relates to sexual activity but also our behavior as sexual persons?

The relationship between sexuality (specifically sexual activity) and sexual violence is a complex and multidimensional reality which finds expression in numerous areas of our lives. The resulting questions abound. Why is most rape perpetrated by males against females? Why does a man choose to use his penis as a weapon to harm another person? Why are men "supposed" to be sexually aggressive and women sexually passive? Why is so much of the violence inflicted on women and children "sexual" in nature? Why do some people find violence erotic? Why does our society seem to be encouraging the erotization of violence? The tendency of this society to equate or confuse sexual activity with sexual violence is a predominant reality in our socialization, attitudes, beliefs, and behavior. This confusion must be addressed if we are to succeed in halting sexual violence.

Sources of Confusion

The confusion between sexual activity and sexual violence is rooted in a complex set of beliefs that are integral to the process of male and female socialization. They promote and sustain the thinking that there is no difference between sexual activity and sexual violence. This view is so deeply rooted in our culture that it has come to be regarded as a part of human nature. In fact, these beliefs are indicative of a false consciousness which survives because few people are willing to question the norm. The following beliefs support the confusion of sexual violence with sexual activity.

ERRONEOUS BELIEF NO. 1

Anything that employs the sexual organs must be primarily sexual in nature. If I were to approach a good friend and reach out with my hand to touch gently that person's face, that gesture would be interpreted by the person as an act of affection and friendship. If, on the other hand, I approached that person with my hand in a fist and struck him/her on the side of the face, the gesture would be interpreted as an act of hostility and violence. I would be using the same part of my body, my hand, in contact with the same part of the other person's body, the face, and yet I would be acting in antithetical ways toward the other person. Likewise, in sexual activity, a man uses his penis or any other part of his body as a means of giving and receiving sexual pleasure and affection. But in sexual violence he uses the same part of his body as a weapon to violate and assault another person. Just because he is using sexual organs in the process does not mean that his primary motivation is sexual.

Erroneous Belief No. 2

The source of a man's sexual response is external and somehow beyond his control. He is not responsible for what he does with that response. The colloquial expression of this belief is that "men can't control themselves" and its corollary is that women have to be responsible for men's sexual response (i.e., "don't get him turned on or you're in trouble"). If, as the belief goes, even the sight of a woman arouses a man, and if he cannot control his behavior when aroused, then, the belief concludes, if he sexually attacks her it is the woman's fault because she aroused him. More simply, this is known as "blaming the victim." Just because a man is sexually aroused and has an erection does not mean that he has to "put" that erection somewhere, i.e., into another person against her will. He can choose to deal with his sexual feelings in other ways, e.g., masturbation. A woman is not the sole source of heterosexual male arousal. The presence or sight of a woman may be one of many factors leading to arousal, including the individual's socialization and erotic learnings.[1] In no way is she the *cause* and therefore the *object*, willing or unwilling, of his sexual attention. Men do have the capability to be responsible for their sexual feelings and behaviors.

ERRONEOUS BELIEF NO. 3

The widely accepted "romantic love ideal" requires a dominant-subordinate relationship between two people. Florence Rush describes the "prototype of romantic love" as containing the "formula of one dominant and one subordinate partner."[2] For example, as prerequisites for romantic interest between a man and a woman, he must be taller, stronger, and make more money; she must be shorter, weaker, and make less money. Supposedly it is this formula of one up and one down that creates and sustains the erotic and emotional interest in romantic love. In heterosexual relationships, the male is dominant and the female subordinate—an arrangement which is accepted widely by both partners without question.[3] Male sexuality seems to be dependent on always being in a dominant position vis-á-vis a subordinate sexual partner, or as Susan Griffin observes, "male eroticism is wedded to power."[4]

The connection of male dominance with male eroticism was clear to me in a conversation I had with a male colleague about sexual assault. I asked him to think of a way in which he could identify with a rape victim. He proceeded to describe an occasion when a female sexual partner had taken the initiative in sexual activity which had the result of immediately diminishing his erotic interest in her. He did not like what he regarded as her "sexual aggression" toward him. First, my colleague mistakenly identified his experience as parallel to a woman's experience of sexual assault. He equated his partner's sexual initiative with the assaultive aggression of a sex offender. He never imagined himself as actually a victim of sexual *assault* by a man or group of men. He revealed much more about this culture's prescription for male sexuality than he realized. In this and other cultures, male dominance has become eroticized as has its corollary, female submission. Male dominance is the key ingredient for male erotic interest and sexual performance. In order for men to be aroused, they feel that they must be in control of the sexual interaction and that their partner should be passive and submissive. The belief is that together dominance and submission and power and powerlessness create the formula which sparks erotic desire in both men and women.

In our society, women and children fulfill the subordinate status necessary to complement male dominance and thus are vulnerable targets for exploitation and abuse. Rush suggests that this dominant-subordinate pattern helps explain why men sexually abuse both women and children: "Since both women and children have been lumped together as helpless, dependent, and powerless, they even share the same 'feminine' gender and consequently both have been sexually abused by men."[5] Any time there is an imbalance of power between individuals or groups of persons, there is the real potential for abuse of the less powerful by the more powerful. If the romantic love ideal in our society is posited on a dominant-subordinate relationship between persons, then it is no surprise that sexual activity and sexual violence have become confused.

ERRONEOUS BELIEF NO. 4

Men have the prerogative to impose their sexuality on others regardless of others' wishes. As a corollary to the "romantic love ideal," men's supposed sexual prerogative is the basis of male sexuality as it is experienced in this culture. At the heart of male sexuality, according to James Nelson, is a sexist dualism which posits the norm of male superiority over female inferiority.[6] It is the established norm in this society that men have more power than women in all relationships, including sexual ones. The power of the male is what gives him the prerogative to take what he wants sexually. The powerlessness of the female forces her to submit to his wishes and desires, or to use covert means to gain some power in the relationship. Coercion and manipulation become accepted

means of interaction. Male sexuality begins to appear predatory in nature, i.e., it takes what it wants when it wants it
without regard for the consequences to others.

Male sexuality as defined by the dominant culture includes
the following elements:

- a desire that its object be "innocent," i.e., powerless,
  passive, subordinate;
- a need to *objectify* the other in order to avoid intimacy;
- a desire to *use* another person exclusively to meet
  one's own needs;
- an ability to *rationalize* the experience: "she likes it,
  wants it, needs it; it's good for the kids . . .";
- a lack of regard for the other as an autonomous person;
- a lack of responsibility for one's acts; no one makes any
  demands or requires any form of accountability;
- an inability to find erotic/emotional pleasure with an
  equal, male or female, or with someone who takes the
  initiative sexually;
- a sexual orientation which is predatory and dependent
  on the subordination of the partner;
- an avoidance of rejection by always being in control.

These aspects of culturally defined male sexuality occur in
varying degrees and combinations in most men in our society.
They are also characteristic of sex offenders and child molesters. To the extent that these characteristics have become the
norm for male sexuality, sexual activity and sexual violence
have become thoroughly confused.

Theologically, the second and third chapters of Genesis, as
it has traditionally been interpreted and generally accepted,[7]
provides support for this understanding of male sexuality.
According to this interpretation of the story, man was created
first and superior. Then God created woman from man's rib
for the sake of man; she was created to serve his needs and so

that he should not be lonely anymore. This understanding of woman's creation underlies the primary assumptions that woman's role is first and foremost to serve man. Woman's job, as the story goes, is to meet man's needs.

The idea that women were created in and of themselves as separate and equal persons who have needs, gifts, and reasons for being outside of relationships with men is absent in this interpretation. The first chapter of Genesis, however, provides a view of the co-equal creation and co-equal responsibility of woman and man. Woman and man are created simultaneously in this version: God created humankind, male and female. Unfortunately, this creation story is not the one which has most affected our cultural or theological beliefs regarding men, women, and sexuality.

As long as erroneous beliefs about male sexuality go unchallenged, the confusion between sexual activity and sexual violence will remain a predominant reality in our society and will continue to support the conditions which encourage sexual violence. What is most disturbing is the growing tendency to identify male eroticism with violence. The confusion may well become reality; sexual violence may become the norm of sexual activity. As violence becomes eroticized, "in the spectrum of male behavior, rape, the perfect combination of sex and violence, is the penultimate act."[8] The erotization of violence means that the acts of violence and abuse themselves bring sexual arousal for men. The object of the act of violence is almost always a woman or child. This tendency is apparent in commercial sexually explicit materials, in the increasing number of horror films complete with female victims, in advertising, in contemporary music, etc. The media now both reflects and encourages the erotization of violence. (See Chapter 12, "Strategies for Action.")

In discussing pornography, psychoanalyst Robert Stoller comments that "An essential dynamic in pornography is hostility. . . . One can raise the possibly controversial question whether in humans (especially males) powerful sexual excitement can ever exist without brutality also being present."[9] In response to Stoller, Irene Diamond suggests that "Stoller has recognized the complexity of the prevailing pattern of male 'sexual' behavior in patriarchal society, but he has not acknowledged the possibility that the 'natural' dynamic may in fact be structured by patriarchy."[10] We can only hope that Diamond is correct. Otherwise, we are left with the fatalistic belief that male sexuality *is* by nature violent and abusive, and that male sexual desire *is* dependent on the subordination of another.

Growing Up Confused

Our earliest socialization teaches us to confuse sexual activity with sexual violence. From the beginning we learn attitudes and patterns of behavior which are based on this confusion. Any effort in later life to understand and distinguish between the two goes against the dominant socialized pattern.

Many women grow up with the adages "boys will be boys" and "men are just like that" as significant learnings in their sexual socialization. Translated, these mean that males are naturally aggressive, not trustworthy, will take advantage of women sexually; and there's nothing to be done about it because that's "just the way men are." For example, girls learn that, unlike them, adolescent males have an uncontrollable sex drive and that all men really want from women is sex. Inherent in these messages is a deep suspicion of male behavior which is not altogether unfounded.

During adolescence, girls learn about "romance" and/or sex watching movies and television, listening to the radio, and reading magazines and books. Here the message is double-edged. They learn to desire a romantic, sentimental love relationship *and* to expect a sexually aggressive male who is in control of the social/sexual interaction. The two become easily confused in the girls' experience: In order to have the romance, they learn to accept the aggression.

In the face of a sexually aggressive male, "nice" girls say "no" and a few "nice" boys respect that "no." "Good" girls never say "yes." Sexuality education for girls in Catholic schools frequently focused on the lesson based on St. Maria Goretti, the young woman who was martyred as she resisted the attack of a rapist.[11] For girls, the message was that it was better to give up one's life than one's virginity. The secondary messages were equally important. A female's technical virginity takes precedence over her life; her value as a sexual object is more important than her personhood and survival; sexual activity is violent and aggressive and woman's role is to resist and defend her virginity. The confusion between sexual activity and sexual violence is powerfully instilled in this teaching. A more valuable teaching would have been to accurately portray Maria Goretti as a rape victim who attempted to defend herself from attack, and then to distinguish between this and a sexual relationship based on consent and respect. This lesson would help correct the confusion perpetuated in the dominant culture.

Growing up, many girls find themselves the object of sexual advances from adult males. They learn quickly that seldom does an adult believe their reports of molestation, nor do adults protect them from other adults. For example, a girl child's veiled reference to Uncle Harry's fondling of her brings, not protection, but punishment for "making up bad stories." Women learn very early that sex is something *done to* them by a male, that their proper sexual role is passivity, and that they have no right to determine what happens to them sexually. From an early age many women experience themselves as powerless sexual objects. As they become adults, they learn that they should appreciate this position of passivity. In *Gone With the Wind*, Rhett Butler forcefully carries a resisting Scarlett O'Hara up the stairs to a bedroom rape from which she awakens smiling happily. Women learn that forced sexual activity is something to be accepted *and* enjoyed. They learn that sexual activity is an area of their lives over which they have little control.

Both women and men are taught that "women say 'no' when they mean 'yes,'" i.e., women say "no" to male sexual advances even when they really want to engage in sexual activity because they are afraid to admit their own sexual desires and needs. In other words, both men and women learn that relating to each other is a game which by necessity involves manipulation and coercion.[12] For males, inherent in all the messages they receive is a deep suspicion of female behavior. Men are taught that women will manipulate them to get what they want; they learn that women cannot be trusted because they often do not play the game fairly. Women must be kept at an emotional distance or else they will take over a man's life and he will lose control of the situation. Unfortunately, women do play the game, often in order to survive. They play the passive role to the man's aggressive role. They do not always take responsibility for their own sexual desires and thus on occasion do say "no" when they want to say "yes." But for her to do otherwise would mean being labelled a "loose woman" or would so threaten her male partner that he would bid her farewell. That risk is often too great for many women. So the game continues.

Many men also grow up with the adages "boys will be boys" and "men are like that" as significant learnings in their sexual socialization. Translated these mean that males are naturally aggressive (and have permission to be so), are always in control of a situation, are sexually active with numerous partners, and are not responsible for their own actions. They also learn that virtually any female in any circumstance, public or private, is "fair game." Whether on the street, in the workplace, or in the home, men learn that they have the right of sexual access to almost any woman, i.e., any woman not already spoken for by another male. All they have to do is take the initiative in establishing social contact; women are expected to respond eagerly to their attention. Adolescent boys also are exposed to movies, TV, radio, books, and magazines (including "girlie" magazines and soft/hardcore pornography). They learn through the media that women, as the *objects* of their erotic desires, have to be controlled; and that as men, they are expected to know what they are doing and stay in control of the other person.[13] Women, they are taught, like a strong man to take charge; women like to be sexually ravished and abused; women prefer men who take control of them. Some boys also experience sexual advances by adults—males and/ or females. Since, like girls, they learn that no one will protect them from this exploitation, they resolve early on that they will never allow themselves to be in such a powerless position again. Rather than be exploited they learn to exploit.

As a result, male sexuality in our culture is presented and experienced as something possessive, aggressive, hostile, harsh, violent, controlling, and with little hint of tenderness, gentleness, mutuality, or respect.[14] This is not to say that all men in our culture have accepted this norm. However, the manifestations of this male image dominate media, advertising, business, politics, etc. Men are provided with a macho ideal in John Wayne, Clint Eastwood, Al Pacino, Richard Roundtree, Mick Jagger, Fred Williamson, the Marlboro Man, and others. They are told that to be a "real man" means to be tough and in control, socially and sexually. For those who *have* accepted this norm, violence is the ultimate means of proving one's manhood whether on the football field, in the tavern brawl, at the diplomatic conference table, or in confrontation with one's spouse. Subtle and overt violence becomes the means by which men stay in control. A man's masculinity and sexuality become tied to violence.

Bernie Zilbergeld writes of this reality in *Male Sexuality:*

> With all the grinding and slamming and banging portrayed in the media, and with the absence of good examples of more tender lovemaking, it is not surprising that many men think of sex as a rough and tough business and that they will be most appreciated if they pummel the hell out of their partners. Since women in fantasyland are always grateful to the most aggressive and even violent lovers, and since there is a clear implication that a man who cannot brutalize a woman is something less than a man, there is considerable pressure for a man to restrain his more tender expression of affection and give free rein to his more aggressive tendencies.[15]

The confusion of sexual activity with sexual coercion and violence has become the core of male sexual socialization. The implications for society are far-reaching as Nelson points out:

> A certain code of masculinity is purchased at the price of suppressing tenderness and self-acceptance. Socialized toward a deep fear of homosexuality and toward a self-respect based in considerable measure upon sexual potency and conquest, the young man is torn by both cultural demands and fear about his own sexual strength. The implications for social violence are unmistakable.[16]

More importantly for this discussion, the implications of sexual violence for all people are unmistakable. Women, as the objects of male efforts to prove their manhood, pay a high price. The resulting homophobia[17] victimizes lesbians and gay men who become the objects of harassment, discrimination, and overt violence in the form of "queer bashing." And finally, all men experience the profound alienation from self, from others, and from nature that produces truncated persons motivated by fear, whose only real power lies in their potential to do violence to others and who represent a danger to all of society.

Examples of Confusion

Manifestations of the confusion of sexual activity with sexual violence abound in our cultural attitudes and practices. Examples of this confusion help to clarify its nature and its consequences, particularly for victims of sexual violence.

• Individual attitudes often suggest that victims of rape or child molestation must have done something "sexual" to entice or provoke the offender.

> When a 15-year-old boy raped a girl in a stairwell at West High School, Judge Archie Simonson ruled, he was reacting "normally" to prevalent sexual permissiveness and women's provocative clothing. . . . The 16-year-old victim was wearing tennis shoes, blue jeans and a blouse over a turtleneck sweater when she was attacked by three boys.[18]

It matters not whether the victim was age 10 months, 5, 25, or 75 years old. The suspicion lingers that since she was attacked or abused, she must have been "being sexual." In fact, her *vulnerability* (at any age) allowed her to be attacked or abused. But the cause of the attack is with the attacker who was not primarily sexually motivated.

• Advertising has recently discovered that not only does sex sell, but sex combined with violence sells even better. There is currently a sharp increase in the use of images which use sex and violence. For example, there was a photo on the cover of a record album of a sexy, glamorous woman who has been beaten black and blue and is tied up with ropes, with the caption stating that she loves to be beaten. Advertising for fashions and records and tapes frequently uses the sex-violence theme. Unfortunately, it is selling more than just the product; it is selling the confusion between sexuality and violence.

• The use of sodomy laws to prosecute male-on-male rape is yet another example of the confusion between sexual activity and sexual violence. Traditionally, sodomy laws were created to discourage homosexual activity between consenting adult males. According to these laws, sodomy or anal intercourse under any circumstances was illegal. Because most of the old rape laws specified that rape was something which men did to women only, those laws could not be used to prosecute same-gender rape. Instead, sodomy laws, which originally had only dealt with sexual activity rather than sexual assault, have been used to prosecute male-on-male rape. It is as if the real offense in male-to-male rape is the same-gender sexual contact rather than the assault which has taken place. Since rape of a male by a male is sexual violence, the laws pertaining to sexual assault should be used in its prosecution. This is the case under many of the newer sexual assault statutes.

• The traditional interpretation of Scripture has often been shaped by the confusion of sexual activity with sexual violence. The clearest example of this is the Sodom and Gomorrah story (which is retold in a more complete version as the story of the Levite and his concubine in the nineteenth chapter of Judges). These are stories about the threatened (and, in Judges, the actual) sexual attack on guests spending the night in a strange town. Yet these stories have virtually always been interpreted in Christian tradition as referring to homosexual contact.[19] This misinterpretation and its influence on Christian teaching has resulted in silence on the sin of sexual violence and inaccurate information and confused ethical teaching on homosexuality.

• Similarly in Christian sexual ethics, there traditionally has been an over-emphasis on the form of sexual activity, i.e., the who, what, when, and where; and almost no emphasis on the context of sexual activity, i.e., the power relationship between the two persons and the presence or absence of consent. For example, sexual activity outside of marriage is considered wrong; and sexual activity inside of marriage is considered right no matter what the circumstances. This avoids the reality that marriage *per se* does not mean that sexual activity within it will be consensual and respectful. It well may be in fact coercive and abusive, but in the eyes of the Church such sexual activity is permitted because official marriage legitimizes it. The confusion between sexual activity and sexual violence has encouraged this ethical morass.[20]

• Frequently, under some rape laws, a defense attorney can use the victim's past sexual history as a means of discrediting the victim and undermining the prosecution of the rapist. If the defense suggests that the victim was sexually active prior to the assault, then it can try to convince the jury that the victim really is a "loose" woman who frequently "gives away" her sexual attentions and that this "alleged" rape is really only another incidence of the same. Inherent in these laws is the idea that any woman who is sexually active outside of marriage is unrapable: She cannot be raped because she freely gives away sex. The failure here to distinguish between what is consenting sexual activity and what is sexual violence puts the victim at a disadvantage and often results in the acquittal of the rapist. Fortunately, some of the new rape laws specify that a victim's past sexual history cannot be used as evidence unless there are extenuating circumstances. These laws differentiate between consenting sexual activity and sexual violence.

• Similarly, it has been held that prostitutes cannot be raped because they are always sexually available. The only possible offense against them might be a customer who got something for nothing but then that, of course, would not be considered rape but theft. In fact a prostitute can be raped. Even though she may agree to provide sexual services for a fee, that does not mean that she is available for sexual assault against her will. The difference between willingly providing sexual service as a form of consenting sexual activity and being the victim of assault must be clarified. Because of the confusion, prostitutes are highly vulnerable to sexual and physical assault and usually have little legal recourse when rape occurs.

• Some still believe that rape is a sexual event for the victim as well as the rapist. This attitude is evident in a recent public comment made by a Spokane, Washington, police captain who was asked what advice he would give to women concerned about an increasing number of rapes in the area. His response was "Lay back and enjoy it."[21] In his mind, there appears to be no difference between sexual activity and sexual violence.

Confusion Explained: A Choice of Continuums

There are two ways of looking at the relationship between sexual violence and sexual activity. In the past, rape has been viewed as the extreme expression of sexual activity. On Continuum I it appears thus:

Continuum I

"normal"
sexual activity ————————————————————|——— rape

This drawing illustrates the definition of rape as "just sex that got out of hand." Somewhere on this continuum there is a line which delineates where sex stops and rape begins. While there is no real agreement as to where that line falls relative to specific behaviors, it would appear that the delineation has something to do with force. Sexual activity is considered normal as long as it takes place without overt physical force; it becomes rape when one partner physically forces the other in an overt way. The logical implication of this paradigm is that rape is an extreme form of sexual activity in which overt force is used when a man cannot control his sexual drive or because a woman resists his sexual attention.

A second way of looking at the relationship between sexual violence and sexual activity makes a clear distinction between the two and suggests a normative statement on the nature of sexual activity. In order to illustrate both the nature of and the distinctions between sexual activity and sexual violence, Continuums II and III must be considered together. These continuums make it clear that there is a similar range of human experience and behavior within both and yet a difference between them. Obviously there is more than one style of sexual activity and more than one type of sexual violence. There are degrees of force within sexual violence and degrees of initiative/receptivity within sexual activity. But the two continuums are mutually exclusive. In this paradigm, sexual activity is by definition consensual and takes place in a context of mutuality, respect, equality, caring, and responsibility. Sexual violence involving either adults or children is antithetical to this definition of sexual activity. Sexual violence is by definition nonconsensual and takes place in the context of exploitation, hostility, and abuse.

Continuum II illustrates the escalation of aggression.

Continuum II: Sexual Violence (nonconsensual)

coercive
"sex"[22] ——————————————————————————— rape

For purposes of clarification, the extremes of Continuum II are marked "coercive 'sex'" and "rape." The extreme form of sexual violence labelled "rape" is easy to identify: A woman is kidnapped from a parking garage, taken to an abandoned house, beaten, and is subjected to oral and vaginal sexual assault by two men. They then lock her in the trunk of her car, take her to a strange part of town, and leave her with no

clothing. No one could fail to see that this incident was anything but rape: a physical and sexual attack which was unwar-
ranted and unprovoked.

The other end of the continuum, which is labelled "coercive 'sex,'" is less easy to identify. For example, a woman goes
out on her second date with a man she met through a friend.
She likes him and is possibly interested in developing an
ongoing relationship. Toward the end of the evening he in-
vites her to his apartment and upon arrival there, asks her to
go to bed with him. She says no, she prefers not to, but
maybe another time. He persists, reminding her that he
bought her an expensive dinner and expects something in
return; then he gets physically aggressive. She submits to
sexual intercourse. Afterwards, he feels some sexual satisfaction but an emotional void. But then sex is like that for him.
She feels used and confused. But then men are like that, she
thinks. Besides, maybe this means he really does like her and
is interested in seeing her again. Many people would argue as
to whether or not this was sexual violence. She does not think
of herself as a victim although she feels many of the same
things that victims of rape feel. He does not think of himself as
a rapist although he feels many of the same things that a rapist
feels. For both of them this encounter is probably interpreted
as a minor skirmish in the war between the sexes and, though
disappointing, it represents yet another confirmation that
"this is what sex is really all about anyway." Yet using the
criteria cited earlier for distinguishing sexual activity and sexual violence, it is clear that this incident belongs on the sexual
violence continuum and not on the sexual activity one.

Most sexual violence occurs on the "coercive 'sex'" side of
the continuum and much of this is not recognized and/or
reported as such. Victims are more likely to report a rape that
is clearly a rape both by legal and cultural definitions. If victims are confused themselves about what occurred, or fear
that they will not be believed, or that they will be blamed for

the incident, they are unlikely to report it. Unfortunately, for many persons, especially children and teenagers, the only "sexual" experience they have had has been coercive or violent. For them, it is easy to come to the conclusion that sexual activity *is* by nature coercive and violent, something over which they have no control. This experience provides the basis for their confusion between sexual activity and sexual violence.

Continuum III provides a way of describing sexual activity in contrast to sexual violence.

Continuum III: Sexual Activity (consensual)

receptive   pro-active[23]
sexual activity   sexual activity

It illustrates the range of differences that a person experiences in sexual activity described as more or less pro-active or receptive. When two people share a sexual encounter, one person may be more pro-active and the other more receptive. One takes the initiative and suggests or begins sexual activity. The other decides whether or not to consent and, if consenting, receives the sexual attention of the partner and participates freely in the sexual interaction. These pro-active and receptive stances often shift back and forth during the sexual sharing so that each person is both pro-active and receptive depending on their mood and desire. Frequently in heterosexual activity, sexual sharing is limited to gender roles: The male is expected to be active and take the initiative; the female is expected to be receptive and wait for the male. Fortunately these limited expectations need no longer restrict sexual activity. The traditional gender roles are not particularly fulfilling for either the woman or the man. He is under pressure to take the initiative and to perform sexually, satisfying not only his own needs but hopefully those of his partner as well. She is expected to wait for his initiative, dependent on his performance to satisfy her and unable to express or fulfill her own sexual needs.

Sometimes one person prefers to be primarily receptive and finds sexual satisfaction in the initiative and active stance of his/her partner. At other times, the opposite may be true. A satisfying sexual encounter takes into account the flux of receptive and pro-active desires. What is important to realize about this continuum of sexual activity as it is defined here is that sexual activity is not without powerful and intense physical expression. It is the giving and receiving of sexual pleasure and satisfaction which is often passionate. However, this understanding of sexual activity is to be distinguished from "coercive 'sex.'" The "pro-active" stance in sexual activity is markedly different from the "coercive" behavior in "coercive 'sex.'" In the pro-active stance, one person initiates sexual activity and proceeds *only* with the consent of the other. In the coercive role, one person initiates sexual activity and proceeds regardless of the lack of consent.

The two continuums of sexual violence and sexual activity are mutually exclusive and do not intersect. As the discussion suggests, they are separate and distinct experiences. The distinction is both qualitative and ethical. One who experiences sexual activity feels different than one who experiences sexual violence. In sexual activity both parties feel affirmed, respected, empowered, and reassured as they share emotional and physical intimacy. In an encounter characterized by sexual violence, the victim feels fear, powerlessness, exploitation, confusion, and a sense of being out-of-control as sexual contact is imposed with no intimacy. The offender feels powerful, in control, hostile, and dominant. At the same time he lacks self-esteem and self-confidence and feels little sexual satisfaction.

Ethically, sexual activity and sexual violence are categorical opposites based on the presence or absence of consent. "Consent" in this instance refers to the informed and freely chosen agreement to engage in sexual activity. "Consent" should be distinguished from "submission" which refers to yielding to the power or authority of another. This distinction is important in understanding the difference between sexual activity and sexual violence. On occasion a rape or an incest victim will submit without struggle or resistance to the sexual attack or abuse. However, this is very different than consenting to sexual contact. Consent requires that a person have all the necessary information to make a decision and the power to choose and have that choice respected by others. Thus, a 5-year-old who has neither information about sexuality nor power vis-á-vis an adult is forced to submit to sexual activity with that adult. A teenager may have sufficient information about sexuality but not have power vis-á-vis her/his father or employer; thus she/he is forced to submit. An adult who has both sufficient information about sexuality and the power of consent may verbally and physically resist a rapist until the rapist's physical force and/or a weapon overpower her/him and force submission.

The area of greatest difficulty for many people in trying to understand their sexual experiences and experiences of sexual violence or abuse focuses on the fine line that often exists between consent and nonconsent. For example, does a woman ever really consent or just submit? This is an especially difficult area for women who have, up until recently, never been allowed to see themselves as sexual persons. Having been well-trained to say "no" even when they want to say "yes," how can they know if their "no" is really a "no" or if their "yes" is really a "yes"? Or how do persons who are sexually inexperienced and struggling to explore their own sexuality choose when to consent and when to withhold consent?

The fine line between consent and nonconsent often focuses on the notion of seduction, regarded by some as a polite form of acquaintance rape. Lorenne Clark and Debra Lewis give us a more positive definition in stating that "seduction involves persuading a woman to act according to her own desires and contrary to the duties imposed on her . . ."[24] This definition of seduction helps to clarify the difficulty regarding consent. Persuasion or encouragement to act in accordance with one's desires, even though contrary to traditional roles or expectations, still can fall within the criteria suggested above for sexual activity as opposed to sexual violence. In other words, persuasion is not coercion; persuasion will finally take "no" for an answer while coercion will not. Seduction then means approaching someone who has adequate information about sexuality and the power to consent or refuse and seeking to persuade them to engage in sexual activity. The context remains one of respect, mutuality, equal regard for the welfare of the other, etc.

The other difficult aspect of consent versus nonconsent is: At what point in a sexual encounter does one give consent and can a person change her/his mind later on? "She said she wanted to have sex with me. So we started to mess around. Then when I got aroused, she changed her mind. What was I supposed to do? I couldn't stop then." The fact is that people *do* change their minds and often for no apparent reason. Sexual interaction is no different from any other human interaction. For example, a person decides to buy a car and puts money down. At that point, the person consents to the deal made with the seller and promises to purchase the car; however, between the time the down payment is made, the contract is signed, and the purchaser takes delivery, either the buyer or the seller can back out of the deal. If this occurs, the down payment may be lost and one party may be disappointed but it was assumed at the beginning of the deal that consent could be withdrawn at any time prior to delivery. So why do people behave as if *initial* consent to sexual activity is irreversible?

Sometimes consent is withdrawn because the circumstance of the sexual encounter changes. "I agreed to have sex with him, you know, regular sex. I never knew that he meant anal sex too. When he started that, I told him to back off—I wasn't interested. He didn't listen. He said that I promised him sex and that's what he wanted." Again, drawing a parallel with a business transaction helps clarify this situation. Two people enter into a business agreement under specific terms. When those terms are modified by either party, the agreement is void until a new set of terms are negotiated and agreed to. A sexual encounter is similar. If one person agrees to a particular type of sexual activity and the other person modifies the form of activity in a way which is not amenable to the first person, then consent may be withdrawn with good reason.

The ethical issues at stake here are complex. The tendency of our society to confuse sexual activity with sexual violence is deeply rooted in our cultural consciousness and profoundly influences our beliefs, feelings, and behaviors related to sexuality. Continuum I illustrates the confusion between "normal" sexual activity and rape. In fact it is a juxtaposition of Continuums II and III. In this confused view, sexual activity becomes subsumed under sexual violence and any meaningful distinction between the two is lost: violence becomes erotic and "good" sex is violent. Continuums II and III are used to illustrate the distinction between sexual activity and sexual violence in order to support our claim that there *is* a difference between the two, and to establish ethical norms based on this distinction.

If we believe that the focus of erotic interests is the result of learning and socialization, then it is no surprise that sexual activity has become confused with violence. When we agree that this development is not in our best interest as a society, we can more effectively name the source and address its cause. When we begin to redefine and differentiate sexual activity from sexual violence, we can achieve the *erotization of equality,* i.e., both women and men will find erotic pleasure in approaching each other as equals, sharing both proactive and receptive sexual activity. With this alternative, we can begin to repair the damage which has been done to women and men by the confusion of sexual activity with sexual violence. (See Chapter 12, "Strategies for Action.")

It All Depends on Your Perspective

Whether sexual violence is seen as an extreme expression of sexual activity (Continuum I) or as a completely different category of human experience (Continuum II) depends on one's view of sexuality.

• If a person begins with the notion that sexual activity is always coercive; that in heterosexual activity, the male must take initiative and control the experience; that women really were created to service men, sexually and otherwise; and that the measure of manhood is determined by aggression and dominance in bed, then it is only logical that sexual violence be seen as the extreme form of sexual activity.

• If one begins with the notion that sexual activity is by its nature coercive; that it is something done to one person by another person without regard for the wishes of the first; that it is something over which one has no control; and that women are expected to provide for men's sexual needs whenever and wherever it is requested if they expect to be supported and accepted by men, then it is only logical that sexual violence be seen as the extreme form of sexual activity.

• If, on the other hand, one believes that sexual activity should always be consensual and take place in a context of respect, equal regard for one another, mutuality, choice, equality and caring; that it is a shared experience which is mutually satisfying; and that any form of force or abuse negates that satisfaction, then it is only logical that sexual violence will be seen as antithetical to sexual activity.

• If a man has experienced women as being passive, shallow, emotionally demanding, manipulative, aggressive, oversexed or undersexed, clearly needing a man to protect them, and secretly wanting to be ravished and needing to be controlled "for their own good"; and if he has never imagined what it would be like to be overpowered by a man and sexually victimized, then he will probably see rape as "sex that got out hand."

• If a woman's first and possibly only subsequent "sexual" experiences have ranged from coercive to violent; and if she has never been in a situation where a man treated her with respect as an equal, she will probably assume that sex *is* coercive and violent because that is the way men are and sexual violence is just more of the same.

• However, if a person has experienced sexual activity which was consensual, respectful, caring; if that person has observed men and women relating to each other with real respect and consideration; and if that person knows that she/he can be a victim of coercive, abusive sexual violence which runs counter to everything they believe about how persons should and can relate to each other, then that person will probably see sexual violence as antithetical to fulfilling and mature sexual activity.

Our attitudes and experiences dramatically shape our perceptions of sexual violence. Likewise new information and/or experiences can change our perceptions. In any case, our perceptions of the nature of sexual violence, the nature of sexuality, and the relationship between the two has a significant impact on our ethical perspective. This effort to reframe the ethical questions surrounding sexual violence begins with the premise that sexual violence and sexual activity are antithetical experiences.

Notes

1. See Bernie Zilbergeld, "Learning About Sex," in *Male Sexuality* (Boston: Little, Brown, and Co., 1978), pp. 12–20.
2. Florence Rush, *The Best Kept Secret—Sexual Abuse of Children* (Englewood Cliffs, N.J.: Prentice-Hall, Inc., 1980), p. 170.
3. In gay or lesbian relationships the same romantic love prototype may function which requires artificial gender roles (butch-femme) to be imposed in order to create and sustain a subor-

dinate–dominant relationship.

4. Susan Griffin, *Rape: The Power of Consciousness* (San Francisco: Harper & Row, 1979), p. 7.

5. Rush, p. 170.

6. James Nelson, *Embodiment* (Minneapolis, Mn.: Augsburg Publishing House, 1978), p. 46.

7. See Phyllis Tribble, *God and the Rhetoric of Sexuality* (Philadelphia: Fortress Press, 1978), pp. 12–23.

8. Griffin, p. 7.

9. Laura Lederer, ed., *Take Back the Night* (New York: William Morrow and Company, Inc., 1980), p. 203.

10. *Ibid*.

11. See Chapter 3, "Reframing the Ethical Questions."

12. In *The Intimate Enemy—How to Fight Fair in Love and Marriage*, Bach and Wyden prescribe the game to their readers: "And some women like to resist and protest too much. When they say 'no, not now,' they really mean 'Yes if' (you really passionately want me). Then such a wife can give herself to the rapist [her husband] and say 'I'm overcome by you.' . . . Men should not simply assume that their partners don't at times feel like being raped; and that 'no' can mean 'yes' if the pursuit is persistent, skillful and genuinely passionate" (p. 262). If women so often say "no" when they mean "yes," what do women say when they mean "no"? The authors then point out that: "Women, especially during the uncertainties of seduction and early courtship, will accommodate to the male level of aggression assigned to them. They usually keep secret their own desire for more or less tenderness. . . ." (p. 261). The woman is expected to play the game and is blamed for it at the same time. Finally, the authors reassuringly conclude: "As partners learn how to fuse sex and aggression, their sex satisfaction gradually increases and their need to injure others verbally or physically decreases" (p. 261). In no way is male sexual aggression questioned nor are men held accountable for their sexually aggressive activity. George R. Bach and Peter Wyden, *The Intimate Enemy* (New York: William Morrow and Co., 1969).

13. Dr. Anne Ganley, a therapist who works with violent men, comments: "Men define 'being in control' as having control

over another person or a situation, not as self-control."

14. This passage from Piper's *Biblical View of Sex and Marriage* is an extraordinary statement which reflects a cultural norm for male sexuality and discounts women's objections to this norm because women who object do not know their place: "The fact that erotic personal love and sexual desire are not necessarily connected causes some modern women to look upon sexual intercourse as a degrading experience. They charge that in the sexual relationship they serve only as the means of satisfying a man's sexual appetite. However, this experience is not a universal one. There are women who find full contentment in the fact that they should be physically fit to satisfy a man's passion. On the other hand, it is not accidental that in our days this feeling of degradation should be found especially among educated women with an articulate sense of personal value who engage in extramarital sexual relations" (p. 62). Otto A. Piper, *The Biblical View of Sex and Marriage* (New York: Charles Scribner's Sons, 1960).

15. Zilbergeld, p. 49.

16. Nelson, pp. 66–67.

17. Homophobia is the irrational fear of homosexual feelings in oneself, of lesbians and gay men, and of homosexuality in general.

18. *San Francisco Chronicle*, May 27 and 28, 1977, as cited in Susan Griffin's *Rape: The Power of Consciousness*, p. 86. Following this incident, Judge Simonson was defeated in a recall election and no longer sits on the bench.

19. See Chapter 3, "Reframing the Ethical Questions."

20. *Ibid*.

21. *Spokane Daily Chronicle*, January 8, 1982. This captain, who is responsible for rape investigations, also wore a T-shirt with this comment printed on it. Community groups immediately requested his dismissal but have thus far been unsuccessful.

22. "Sex" is placed in quotation marks here so as to distinguish it from "sexual activity" as it is used in Continuum II.

23. "Pro-active" refers to initiating behavior during sexual activity.

24. Lorenne Clark and Debra Lewis, *Rape: The Price of Coercive Sexuality* (Toronto: The Women's Press, 1977), p. 175.

Chapter 3

REFRAMING THE ETHICAL QUESTIONS

The Ethical Silence

Sexual violence as a topic for ethical discourse among Christians has gone unaddressed. There are many complex reasons for this. One reason certainly is the silence on the topic by society as a whole. Ethicists and pastors, like judges, doctors, police officers, and the general public, have paid little attention to the problem of sexual violence. Specifically in the Christian community, rape and child sexual abuse have been largely overlooked by most ethicists who have shaped traditional and contemporary ethical discussion.

Some might explain the conspicuous absence of ethical reflection on sexual violence by saying that there is no need for it since, like murder, everyone knows and understands that rape is wrong under any circumstance. This explanation is inadequate for two reasons. First, it could be argued that virtually everyone knows and understands that rape is wrong. Yet there is no consensus as to exactly what rape is or what can be defined as sexual violence; and since there is no agreement as to the nature of crimes of sexual assault and child sexual abuse, there is really no unanimous condemnation of sexual violence. Everyone does *not* agrée that sexual violence is wrong under any circumstance; hence there is insufficient community pressure to limit its occurrence. Second, collective agreement on a social norm condemning anti-social acts does not preclude the need for ethical discourse. The example of murder again makes this clear. Even though we can posit some collective agreement that murder is wrong, there is still an abundance of discussion among ethicists and pastors on this issue, for example, in the controversies surrounding capital punishment, nuclear arms, the just war theory, non-violent versus violent social change. If, as a society, we shared a collective understanding and condemnation of sexual violence (which we do not), this still would not be an adequate reason to refrain from ethical discussion of the matter. The most significant reason for the silence in ethical discourse is that sexual violence is something which is perceived to happen primarily to women and children and, as such, has not been a priority for most ethicists. The limitations of a patriarchal bias and male experience (which for most male ethicists probably did not include sexual assault) have meant that sexual violence as an experience and as an ethical issue has been overlooked.

As Christians, we need a clear and unflinching understanding of the ethical and theological dimensions of sexual violence to provide us with the foundation for both a pastoral and political/social response to the problem. In both the Good Samaritan story and in Jesus' reminder that as we do to the least of our sisters and brothers, we do also to him, we find a generic mandate to give aid to the injured. However, this mandate is not sufficient when we are faced with a lack of clarity as to what is the injury and who is the injured. Such is the case with sexual violence. While this generic mandate may call forth a response of compassion, what in the Christian tradition challenges us to a response of justice? How are we to understand and interpret sexual violence as an experience of suffering in light of our faith? How does the relationship between sexuality and sexual violence affect our understanding of Christian sexual ethics? How has our understanding of Christian sexual ethics contributed to our unresponsiveness to sexual violence? The harsh reality of sexual violence requires a comprehensive re-examination of theological sources including Scripture, traditional Christian sexual ethics, and specific Christian teachings about sexual violence. This critical examination will lead us to reframe the ethical questions posed by the experience of sexual violence. We can then develop the ethical and theological foundation which is fundamental to an effective and meaningful response to sexual violence, one which is grounded in the Christian faith.

Scriptural Sources on Sexual Violence

Contemporary attitudes about sexual violence are deeply rooted in our Western cultural heritage. Many of these attitudes are evidenced in the blame we place on the victim, the stereotype of the woman who cries rape falsely, and the confusion of sexual activity and sexual violence. These attitudes have contributed heavily to the inability of society and church to deal realistically with sexual violence. They find, if not their source, certainly their reinforcement in Scripture.

There are, in fact, a number of references to rape and sexual abuse in the Bible. Unfortunately, the best known references convey erroneous information and attitudes about sexual violence. For example, the story of Potiphar's wife has become the prototype of the woman who cries rape falsely. Those stories which *are* accurate in their portrayal are either seldom referred to or misinterpreted. The story of Susanna, a victim of attempted rape who is falsely accused of fabricating her charge by her would-be rapists, is virtually unknown to most Christians. The story of the concubine who is raped and murdered in the nineteenth chapter of Judges is consistently misinterpreted. Sometimes the portrayal is accurate but the sexual offense is passed over as incidental to the story: The incestuous rape in the story of the rape of Tamar is overshadowed by the violation of Tamar's father's property rights. Likewise in the story of Dinah, her rape sets off an extended war between two tribes. It is clear from the passages that the confusion about the nature of sexual violence was well-entrenched in the Hebrew and early Christian culture which produced these stories and laws. On the one hand, they treat crimes of sexual assault as property violations and as primarily sexual in nature; on the other hand, they compare it with murder. The message is inconsistent.

The scriptural references to sexual violence are either stories or laws. The stories are teaching stories. They convey information, attitudes about and an analysis of the experience of sexual violence to make a moral point. Unfortunately, sometimes the moral teaching is misplaced because the analysis and understanding of the experience is confused. The specific Deuteronomic laws regarding acts of sexual assault spell out penalties for offenders and also for victims of sexual assault under specific circumstances. Again, moral and legal teachings are conveyed in these laws and legal consequences are defined. The confusion of sexual activity and sexual violence is reflected here as well and this makes the utilization of Scripture for ethical reflection about the problem of sexual violence even more difficult.

Included here are a series of scriptural passages which reflect teachings from the Jewish and Christian traditions. These will illustrate the difficulty in utilizing Scripture as a source for this ethical discussion.

JOSEPH AND POTIPHAR'S WIFE (GENESIS 39: 1–23)

This is a fairly well-known story about Joseph, the hero, who is a servant to the Egyptian, Potiphar. Joseph was entrusted with the administration of Potiphar's household. Described as handsome, Joseph was invited by Potiphar's wife to come and lie with her. He refused because it would be a sin against God and a betrayal of his master. She insisted and finally one day grabbed his cloak, urging him to have sex with her. Joseph ran away leaving his cloak behind. When her husband returned, she reported to him that Joseph came to her (supposedly to assault her) and that she screamed for help and scared him away. Potiphar was enraged and put Joseph in prison; but even so, "the Lord was with him."

In this classic story of the woman who cries rape falsely, Potiphar's wife has become a prototype of the woman who uses a false charge of rape to get back at an innocent man—here, not only innocent but the hero whom God especially favors.

Potiphar's wife (who is not named) is portrayed as the sexually aggressive female who, because of her class and status, is able to condemn her husband's servant falsely. The teaching is plain: Beware of women crying "rape," especially women with status (in our society, upper-class Caucasians).[1] In reality, false rape charges are a rare occurrence. This story is regarded by many, however, as the "typical rape" with the "typical rape victim" being a vindictive, dishonest woman. This is, in fact, a most atypical situation. Rather than a warning to be aware of false accusations by those in powerful positions, the moral most likely to be remembered is that women falsely accuse men of rape.

SUSANNA (IN THE APOCRYPHA AS "DANIEL AND SUSANNA" OR IN THE CANON AS "DANIEL 13")

This is a virtually unknown story about Susanna, described as a beautiful and devout Hebrew woman. Her husband was a community leader and other community leaders often gathered at their house. Two of these men, respected elders and judges, were "obsessed with lust for her . . ." and came regularly to the house to spy on Susanna as she walked in her garden. One day as they watched, she prepared to bathe in the garden. Seeing her alone, the two men came into the garden and demanded that she "yield" to them. They threatened that if she refused, they would testify that she had been there with a lover and she would be condemned to death. If she submitted, she would be sinning against God. Susanna cried out, refusing to submit. The elders then reported that they found her with a lover and she was put on trial. At the trial, the elders gave their false testimony. Susanna was not permitted to testify at all. The assembly, of course, believed the elders and sentenced her to death. She cried out to God to help her. At this point, God inspired Daniel (the hero) to come to her aid. He questioned the elders' testimony and proved it to be false; then he spoke in judgment of the assailants: "Now we know how you have been treating the women of Israel, frightening them into consorting with you; but here is a woman of Judah who would not submit to your villainy." The elders were sentenced to death. Susanna's innocence was vindicated and Daniel became "a great man among his people."

This is a story which relates to women's experiences of acquaintance rape (assault by someone known and trusted by the victim and her family) and accurately describes the lack of credibility so common for rape victims. This important teaching story, which portrays the double bind of women in the face of sexual assault and gives God's support for vindication, is seldom referred to in contemporary religious teaching. It has been left out of many translations of the book of Daniel. Daniel's strong statement of judgment is a welcome contrast to the preceding story.

Yet the legal limits on women as victims are apparent. Although a victim, she stands accused; she is not even permitted to testify at the trial. Susanna is vindicated only because Daniel defends her. Not only is she the victim of attempted rape and blackmail, but also of the legal system.

This situation has definite parallels with the contemporary legal system. In some states, when a woman reports a rape and the state agrees to prosecute the rapist, the testimony of the victim (as a witness) is inadequate to convict. An additional witness must be able to testify to the events of the rape. This is a legal bind because most rapes occur when the victim is alone. In no other criminal proceedings is a second witness required by law. This legal provision reflects a deep and abiding suspicion that women who report rape cannot be trusted.

THE LEVITE AND THE CONCUBINE (JUDGES 19: 11–30)

This passage is a more detailed version of the Sodom and Gomorrah story. A Levite and his concubine were traveling in a strange part of the country. As night came, they waited in the town square for someone to take them in. (This was the hospitality custom at that time.) An old man welcomed the travelers to his house and gave them supper. As they ate, there was a loud banging at the door. The host answered and was confronted by a gang of men who demanded that the guest be handed over to them that they might have intercourse with him. The host refused and reprimanded the men because to allow any harm to come to his guest would be a serious violation of the hospitality code. Still they demanded, and the host offered instead his virgin daughter and the guest's concubine: "Ravish them and do with them what seems good to you; but against this man do not do so vile a thing." The gang refused the offer. Finally, the guest, growing more anxious, cast out his concubine to them. The gang beat and raped her all night and left her on the doorstep where the guest found her dying the next morning. He put her on his donkey and started home. When he arrived, he cut her body into twelve pieces and sent one piece to each of the tribes of Israel, saying: "Such a thing has never happened . . . from the day that the people of Israel came up out of the land of Egypt; . . . consider it, take counsel, and speak."

The sexual assault described in this story was first threatened by the gang against the male guest and finally inflicted on his concubine. In accepting the concubine, the gang was indirectly assaulting the guest. They destroyed "his" property. It appears that this is what enraged the Levite and the reason he sent the message to the other tribes. There is no importance given to the fact that a woman has been raped and murdered. Never is there further discussion about the host who was willing to sacrifice his own daughter to save his guest. The overriding concern is for the protection of the male guest and the outrage expressed is in response to the destruction of his property.

The story is not about homosexuality. The gang wanted to sexually assault the male guest for the same reason they would rape a woman—to humiliate, overpower, and physically harm the other. When the host refused to allow them to harm his guest, the destruction of the stranger's property (his concubine) was the next best way to violate him. Unfortunately, contemporary interpretation of this story has misused the teaching by focusing on male homosexuality. Little attention has been paid to the fact that the story accurately describes the experience of sexual assault of a woman.

The final outcome of this story follows in the twentieth chapter of Judges when the people of Israel ask the Levite how all of this happened, to which he replies: "I came to Gibeah that belongs to Benjamin, I and my concubine, to spend the night. And the men of Gibeah rose against me, and beset the house round about me by night; *they meant to kill me,* and they ravished my concubine, and she is dead. . . ." While the Levite accurately comprehended the threat against him as one of physical assault, he does not seem to have the same concern for the impact of those acts on his concubine. She remains his property and of a lesser priority. He cut up her body and sent it round because the Benjamites have "committed abomination and wantonness in Israel." (The noun used here also means emptiness and folly and is used similarly earlier in the story by the host to describe the acts threatened by the mob against the guest: "do not do this *vile* thing.") It is apparent that in describing it as an abomination and folly in Israel the community recognized the impact of the assault on its social fabric. Yet the offense that the community is reacting to is the threat to the life and the destruction of the property of one of its male members rather than to the rape and murder of a woman. Because of this offense, which was viewed as an offense against the whole community, "all the men of Israel gathered against the city [of Benjamin], united as one man" and there ensued a major battle in which "the Lord defeated Benjamin before Israel; and the men of Israel destroyed twenty-five thousand one hundred men of Benjamin that day. . ." The men whose property rights had been violated made war on the men who violated them. But the real abomination and folly, the rape and murder of a woman of Israel was never confronted, acknowledged, or vindicated.

THE RAPE OF DINAH (GENESIS 34)

This passage (subtitled the "Seduction of Dinah") introduces Dinah, daughter of Leah and Jacob, on her way "out to visit the women of the land." While she was visiting, Shechem, son of Hamor, saw her; he then "seized her and lay with her and humbled her." Although the text never seems to use a word which can be translated as "rape," this description refers to forced sexual activity which results in humiliation. Following the assault, Shechum expresses love and tenderness to Dinah. He goes to his father, Hamor, and asks him to get Dinah for his wife. Hamor then goes to Jacob to discuss the matter. But Jacob's sons had also heard about what happened to their sister and were angry because Shechem had "wrought folly in Israel by lying with Jacob's daughter, for such a thing ought not to be done." It appears that the folly is that Shechem "lay with" Dinah, i.e. had sexual contact with her, not that he attacked her. In any case, as in Judges 19, the whole community was affected.

But Hamor said: "give your daughters to us, and take our daughters for yourselves" so that they might all live together harmoniously in the land. Hamor and Shechem offered to do anything Jacob asked in exchange. Jacob's sons, seeking to deceive Shechem, agreed only on the condition that he and all the males with him be circumcised. The arrangement was agreed to and all the men of Hamor's tribe were circumcised. Three days later Dinah's brothers attacked the city and killed all the males, including Hamor and Shechem. Then they seized their wives and children along with the rest of their property. Jacob confronted the brothers saying that they had brought trouble on him because the other tribes might now retaliate, but the brothers said, "Should he treat our sister as a harlot?"

The sexual attack on Dinah is the dramatic backdrop for the struggle between Jacob's and Hamor's families. Again the attack is not acknowledged as an offense against Dinah herself, but as a property violation against Jacob and his sons. The response to this violation was collective, vengeful violence. The emphasis in the description is on the sexual nature of the violation: he "lay with her," "defiled her," and treated her as a "harlot." In addition, Shechem was an uncircumcised male and thus not part of the covenant community, hence the "folly in Israel."[2]

At no point is the reader provided with any information about Dinah's experience or reaction to the assault. Neither are we provided with any information about Dinah's life afterwards. Since she lost her virginity and her potential husband was killed by her brothers, what man would have her? And without a man to provide for her, what would happen to her?

THE RAPE OF TAMAR (II SAMUEL 13)

This passage (subtitled "Amnon's Abuse of Tamar") introduces Tamar who is a full sister of Absalom and a half sister of Amnon; all are children of David. In the story, Amnon decided that he loved his sister Tamar, but was distraught because Tamar was "a virgin, and it seemed impossible to

Amnon to do anything to her." So Amnon tricked Tamar into coming to see him, then he grabbed her and told her to lie with him. She refused saying: "do not force me; for such a thing is not done in Israel; do not do this wanton folly." Tamar reminded him that she would be shamed and he would be a fool. She told him to speak to King David who "will not withhold me from you." Ignoring her suggestion and "being stronger than she, he forced her, and lay with her."

Again this is clearly a case of rape, but the violation portrayed is one of property. At that time, it was possible for a man to marry his half-sister, a practice which was later forbidden under the law (see Leviticus 18:9).Yet Amnon refused to request permission from David to marry Tamar perhaps fearing that the request would be rejected. The folly and shame result from Amnon's rape of Tamar without David's permission. In this story, the reader is provided with Tamar's reaction and reminder that she will bear the shame of this attack.

After the rape, Amnon's feelings shifted dramatically to hatred and he sent Tamar away. She confronted him saying that sending her away is an even greater wrong than the assault. Again he ignored her and put her out. Tamar, as a virgin daughter of the king, was wearing a long robe with sleeves. She rent the robe, put ashes on her head, and went away crying. When Absalom saw her he asked if she had been with Amnon. Because it was true, Tamar remained in despair in Absalom's house. When King David heard what happened, he was very angry. Absolom hated Amnon for what he did to Tamar. After two years, Absolom plotted to kill Amnon and commanded his servants to strike Amnon down. Afterwards Absalom fled while David grieved for his son.

Tamar's reaction to her rape is one of public grief and desolation. While this is a common victim reaction to rape, Tamar grieves because she has lost her virginity without gaining a husband to care for her. Because of the property violation she is left without provision; she becomes damaged goods. In fact, as she points out, Amnon does have a responsibility for her.

He refuses though to take that responsibility and thus leaves her in her shame. This is the essence of the offense described here. Yet Tamar's experience is of incestuous assault, i.e., sexual violence done by a family member who tricked her into the situation. Again, the real offense against Tamar herself is overlooked. While we do hear something of Tamar's perspective on the experience, the primary story is of the conflict between brothers; the sexual assault of a woman is incidental. The reaction of her brother Absalom is the traditional act of revenge ending in murder.

While the story makes it clear that the incestuous abuse was destructive to Tamar, her family, and the community and that such a thing should not have been done to her, this judgment is based on the violation of her father's property rights rather than the violation of her personal and civil rights. Because of this sexist bias, the community never attends to the victimization of Tamar *per se* but rather focuses on the economic injury done to her father and brother.

DEUTERONOMIC LAWS (DEUTERONOMY 22: 23–29)

The Old Testament laws address three specific situations of sexual assault and deal with them depending on the circumstances of the situation and the marital status of the victim.

- If a man "lies with" a betrothed virgin *in the city*, both shall be stoned to death: the woman because she did not cry out and the man for violating his neighbor's wife. The assumption here is that if the victim was in the city and cried out, someone would have intervened and prevented the attack. There is no recognition that force or fear may have prevented her screams or that her screams may have gone unheard. So if the attack is carried out without someone intervening, the victim must not have cried for help. This means that she must have eagerly participated in a sexual encounter and thus deserved to die.

- If a man seizes and "lies with" a betrothed virgin *in the country,* only the man shall be killed because although the woman cried out for help, there was no one to save her, "for this case is like that of a man attacking and murdering his neighbor." Only here is the violent nature of the crime emphasized.
- If a man seizes and "lies with" a virgin not betrothed, *and they are found,* the man must give *the father* of the woman fifty pieces of silver and *marry her because he has violated her.*

All of these laws address the sexual assault of a woman as a property crime against the man to whom the woman "belonged," husband or father. Persecution of the victim depends on the locale of the crime and disregards the actual circumstance. If the woman is a virgin and still "belongs" to her father when she is assaulted, the assailant must pay the father restitution and *the victim is condemned to marriage* to her assailant. Consistently these laws regarded rape as a property and sexual crime. The one exception is the reference to the analogy between the rape and murder of a neighbor. Unfortunately, this assessment is overshadowed by the other references.

Some clergy refer to these laws in their pastoral counseling of rape victims to determine whether or not the woman was really raped. "Did you scream? Did you fight back?" become the criteria by which the pastor evaluates the victim's credibility. If she did not scream or fight back, the pastor feels it is his/her task to confront the victim with her sinful condition. (See page 77, "Whose Sin Is This?") This practice betrays a lack of accurate information about rape and insensitivity to the needs of the victim.

LEVITICUS (18: 6–18)

These passages refer specifically to sexual practices of the Hebrews. The prohibitions included here proscribe sexual contact between persons already related by blood since that would amount to "union with one's own flesh."[3] These laws were also intended to separate the Hebrews from their Canaanite neighbors who practiced these sexual activities.

In this passage, the phrase "to uncover the nakedness" of another is used to describe the prohibition:

"None of you shall approach any one near of kin to him to uncover nakedness." "To uncover nakedness" implies some degree of sexual contact which is prohibited because of the close kinship between persons. Types of relationships are specified: son-mother, father-granddaughter, brother-sister, son-father, brother-half sister, nephew-aunt, son-stepmother, father-in-law-daughter-in-law, nephew-aunt by marriage, brother-in-law-sister-in-law. Finally, a man cannot have sexual contact with the daughter or granddaughter of a woman with whom he has had relations. It would appear that this passage is an example of the incest taboo which is often assumed to be universal. Yet there is a conspicuous absence of prohibition against father-daughter or father-son sexual contact. The prohibitions here refer to contact between a male and a female who is the property of someone else.[4] Again the property violation dictates the prohibition of sexual contact. We can speculate that the absence of the father-daughter and father-son prohibitions result from the fact that children were regarded as possessions of their father, which meant that he had sexual license with them. The major concern in these laws is the protection of property from misuse, not the protection of individual persons from exploitation.[5]

In all of the scriptural examples which refer to acts of sexual assault and abuse, the authors are concerned with the offense as a violation of male property rights.[6] We can only assume that the authors' attitudes reflect the views of the community. The one exception to this in the Old Testament/Apocrypha is the story of Susanna in which the attempted rape is discussed as an offense against Susanna herself. The offense is acknowledged and she is vindicated. Yet this chapter was placed in the Apocrypha and not included in the Canon;[7] it certainly is not a well-known story. Its ability to supply a corrective to the perspective of the other Old Testament passages is limited. In addition, even when it does appear, the commentaries discount the emphasis on Susanna's experience of attempted assault.

> Superficially, at least, the primary purpose of the story is to show that virtue (here in the form of conjugal chastity) triumphs, with God's help, over vice (here in the form of lust and deceit). Inasmuch as this story belongs to the "Daniel Cycle," it also offers another example of this hero's God-given wisdom. Exegetes, however, have sought deeper meanings in the tale.[8]

This confusion runs through all of the Old Testament material presented here. In addition, when the passage is misinterpreted and misused, the confusion is compounded. These stories and teachings from the Jewish and Christian traditions are part of our Western cultural heritage and have influenced our society's attitudes about sexual assault and abuse. Much of the distortion about the nature of sexual violence and the treatment of victims is rooted in the Bible. Tracing some of the sources of this confusion and misunderstanding can enable more effective efforts to change cultural and religious attitudes about sexual violence.

NEW TESTAMENT SOURCES

In contrast to the Old Testament, the New Testament does not appear to have any explicit references to sexual violence. However, there are passages which can be utilized to develop a new ethical response to sexual violence. We can look to Jesus' parable of the Good Samaritan for a model of how to respond to the victim if we regard the act of sexual violence as an act of assault and aggression that results in injury. (See Part 2, "A Pastoral Perspective.") In addition, the Gospels consistently regard women as persons in their own right rather than treating them as property. Jesus' ministry was most unusual and puzzling to his followers in that he treated women as persons. Because of this sensitivity, we can assume that victims of sexual violence were not doubly victimized by Jesus' response to them. However, there is no evidence that the confusion of sexual activity with sexual violence had diminished in its influence on the attitudes and practices of the period.

In the New Testament, Jesus discusses "lust" in connection with "adultery." In a passage from Matthew, Jesus suggests that the ethical issue goes beyond the act to the thought and desire which precedes it. "But I say to you that everyone who looks at a woman *lustfully* [emphasis added] has already committed *adultery* [emphasis added] with her in his heart" (Matthew 5:28).

He seems to be saying that the thought and desire to commit a particular act are as significant as the act itself and that persons are as accountable for their thoughts and desires as for their acts. This significant ethical insight is often clouded by traditional interpretation of this passage which has focused on promiscuity. It has been taken to mean that any man who has sexual feelings for a woman is as guilty as if he actually has sexual contact with her.

"Lustfully" means "desiring greatly." "Adultery" was the category used to describe every sexual offense from rape to promiscuity and always referred to the violation of a husband's property rights.[9] So Jesus' literal meaning might more accurately be expressed: "Anyone who desires greatly in his heart to sexually possess a woman has already taken possession of her or stolen her." In other words, he has broken the Commandment which forbids the coveting of another man's wife. Even though this meaning of the verse is still skewed by a patriarchal bias, it brings us closer to the truth than does the traditional interpretation.

Building on this literal meaning, an alternative interpretation of what is meant by "lust" and "adultery" can provide new insight to Jesus' teaching. Rather than understanding "lust" to mean "having sexual feelings," "lust" is used to describe the intense desire *to possess or overcome* another person, particularly sexually. Augustine supports this interpretation: *"The evil of lust, a name which is given to many vices, but is properly attributable to violent sexual appetite* [emphasis added]."[10] This definition corresponds to the previously described dominant cultural understanding of male sexuality as predatory and dependent on domination of the other person. "Adultery" might be understood to refer primarily to an offense against the woman (rather than against her owner) because the consequence of a man's desire to possess and dominate a woman is to break faith by violating mutuality and respect in relation to her.

Thus we can reinterpret Jesus' teaching to mean that for a man to desire to possess and dominate a woman is an offense against her. It is a distortion of human sexuality which is physically and spiritually abusive. Using Jesus' ethical insight that it is not only what one does but also what one thinks that is important and applying it to the contemporary experience of sexual violence enables the reader to interpret the passage in Matthew as emphasizing not promiscuous sexual activity, but rather the potential for sexual coercion and violence in thought, word, *and* deed.[11]

The most useful teaching from Scripture which helps to explain God's response and our responsibility to victims of sexual violence is a concept which is not ordinarily associated with sexual violence *per se*. Widows, fatherless children, travelers, and the poor were designated in the Old Testament as deserving protection and support from the community. If we consider *why* these categories of persons were singled out, we can more easily apply this teaching to our time.

Each of these persons was powerless and vulnerable in their society. The widow and fatherless child (the single-parent family) lacked a male figure to serve as protector, provider, and authority. The sojourner was vulnerable and at a disadvantage because he was traveling outside of his community. The poor lacked the resources to determine their own lives. In patriarchal Hebrew culture, it was assumed that all females were under the authority and protection of a male (father, husband, brother, brother-in-law, etc.) and that male was responsible for providing sustenance and protection for the female. Any woman who was not related to a male in this way was without protection or any livelihood other than prostitution. Thus a widow who had no father, brother, or brother-in-law to take care of her was powerless, vulnerable, and at the mercy of her community.

The Hebrew laws instructed the people to care for the powerless and vulnerable and provide them with food (Deuteronomy 14: 19–22). The prophets frequently chastised the people for their neglect and oppression of these people.

> *Woe to those who decree iniquitous decrees,*
>   *and the writers who keep writing oppression,*
> *to turn aside the needy from justice*
>   *and to rob the poor of my people of their right,*
> *that widows may be their spoil,*
>   *and that they may make the fatherless their prey!*
> *Isaiah 10: 1–2*

> *Wash yourselves; make yourselves clean;*
>   *remove the evil of your doings from before my eyes;*
> *cease to do evil,*
>   *learn to do good;*
> *seek justice,*
>   *correct oppression;*
> *defend the fatherless,*
>   *plead for the widow.*
> *Isaiah 1: 16–17*

If we understand that the concern here was for the powerless and vulnerable, to provide for them and to protect their rights, and if we ask who among us today are powerless and vulnerable and in need of support and advocacy, we would certainly specify the victims of sexual violence, especially women and children. In Hebrew culture, the widow represented the powerless woman who depended on her community to care for her. The contemporary figure might well be the rape victim or child sexual assault victim, both of whom are at the mercy of those around them for support and advocacy.

With this in mind, Jesus' parable about the widow takes on new meaning.

> And he told them a parable, to the effect that they ought always to pray and not lose heart. He said, "In a certain city there was a judge who neither feared God nor regarded the people; and there was a widow in that city who kept coming to him and saying 'Vindicate me against my adversary.' For a while he refused; but afterward he said to himself, 'Though I neither fear God nor regard man, yet because this widow bothers me, I will vindicate her, or she will wear me out by her continual coming.'" And the Lord said, "hear what the unrighteous judge says. And will not God vindicate the elect, who cry to God day and night? Will God delay long over them? I tell you, God will vindicate them speedily. Nevertheless, when the Son of humanity comes, will he find faith on earth?"
>
> Luke 18: 1–8

Here we find Jesus giving assurance that God will vindicate those who cry out. This is then the promise in the New Testament which corresponds to Susanna's experience in the Apocrypha. For the victim, powerless and vulnerable, there is vindication through God.

These new insights from scripture may offer some help in the process of reframing the ethical questions surrounding sexual violence. Although the scriptural material which does address sexual violence is limited in its usefulness, some of the heretofore "unrelated" passages offer additional support for understanding and responding to sexual violence.

The Christian Tradition on Sexual Violence

In order to comprehend the impact of the Christian tradition on our understanding of sexual violence, we must look at the ways that the tradition addresses sexual violence historically and contemporarily. I have selected three historical examples and sampled contemporary sources in order to provide a view of the context in which our religious attitudes and ethical values about sexual violence have developed.

In the Christian tradition, we find only a few direct references to sexual violence. We do, however, find an over-all context which is both patriarchal and often misogynist which contributes heavily to the practice of "blaming the victim." The indirect references within this context are often as significant as the specific ones.

The patriarchal bias of the "Church Fathers" has been carefully examined and documented elsewhere.[12] The misogynist attitudes and practices of individual theologians and church leaders are available *ad nauseam* without apology. These attitudes and practices culminated in the 16th Century with the publication of *Malleus Mallificarum, The Hammer of Witches*. It became one of the basic texts of the Inquisition. The *Malleus* was first printed in 1586 and reprinted at least 29 times until 1669. Though written by Dominicans and supported by the Roman Catholic Church, it was also later adopted by Protestants as their guide to witchcraft.[13] The text describes women as evil, subject to carnal lust, weak, impressionable, defective, impulsive, and liars by nature.[14] Thus, according to this manual, women were susceptible to witchcraft. Given this view of women, it was not difficult to legitimize the organized persecution of women during and after the Inquisition. By merely labelling them witches and thus a seductive danger, church leaders easily justified the torture and murder of thousands of women. The brutal techniques employed in torture included sexual violence and sadism.

> In diabolic intercourse, the devil was believed to place a mark on the witch as the sign that he or she was his property. In women this was normally on the breast or genitals. Small protrusions of the body were also believed to be teats by which the witch nursed her familiar. Witches were stripped and shaved. Their bodies were searched and the sensitive parts pricked in search of these supposed bodily proofs of demonic relations. [15]

Here the church not only was complicit but actively initiated sexual and physical violence against women as punishment for being born female and being labeled "witch."

In fact, it was frequently the case that women and children who were accused of witchcraft were actually victims of sexual violence. Many who "confessed" to fornication with the devil were actually reporting a sexual attack upon them by a man. Rush concludes:

> In a society where sexual abuse went unhampered and people believed in evil spirits, it was not difficult to attribute a sexual offense to a supernatural spirit. [Nicholas] Remy [demonologist and Inquisitor] was satisfied that a child who "could not suffer a man" could accommodate the devil, and in his treatise on demonology he wrote:
>
> > *Although Catherina Latomia of Marche at Haracourt, February 1587, was not yet of an age to suffer a man, he [the devil] twice raped her in prison being moved with hatred for her because he saw that she intended to confess her crime; and she very nearly died of the injuries she received from that coitus.*
>
> Victims of sexual abuse, without a recourse, found it

simpler to blame or even believe that spectral demons
rather than flesh and blood men violated them.[16]

The persecution of women and children as witches provided a
backdrop for the church's response to sexual violence during
the fourteenth to seventeenth centuries. During this period,
the church was not only insensitive to the needs of victims, it
pro-actively persecuted some victims as witches.

There are at least two teachings in the Christian tradition
which directly address the ethical issues surrounding sexual
violence. Both teachings exemplify and perpetuate the confusion of sexual violence with sexual activity. Both address the
question of the nature of the sin of sexual violence.

The first example is an attempt to distinguish between "unnatural" and "natural" sins. It is found in the "moral manuals"
which were used by confessors during the fifteenth to
nineteenth centuries to guide their counsel of parishioners on
sexual matters.[17] These manuals heavily influenced the people's attitudes about sexuality and most of their teachings
promoted "a highly negative, juridical, and act-centered morality, which all too easily proclaimed moral absolutes with
little regard for person-oriented values."[18] A common theme
found in the manuals is the distinction between sexual sins "in
accordance with nature" and those "contrary to nature." The
criterion for natural sexual sins is that the theoretical possibility of procreativity be present, i.e., that a child may be produced. Thus fornication, adultery, incest, rape, and abduction are all regarded as "natural" sexual sins. Although they
are sins, they are less sinful than "unnatural sins." "Unnatural
sins" are masturbation, sodomy, homosexuality, and bestiality. None of these have procreative possibilities; therefore,
they are "unnatural" and as such were considered much more
serious. This hierarchy of sins uses procreation as a criterion
for judging the seriousness of sexual acts. It suggests that
sexual acts, e.g., homosexuality, are in the same category as
sexually violent acts, e.g., abduction and rape. In the natu-

ral/unnatural paradigm, incest, rape, and abduction are considered sinful not because they are in violation of the rights and bodily integrity of the individual, but because they are seen as "sexual activity outside of marriage." These acts are considered less "sinful" than sexual acts which *by their nature* have no victims, for example, masturbation, homosexuality, and bestiality. This paradigm reinforces the confusion of sexual activity with sexual violence by regarding acts of sexual violence as *sexual* sins and seeing their sinful nature as related to sexual *activity* outside of marriage.

The use of procreative criteria as the basis for sexual ethics is an inadequate and counterproductive standard. It results in an "act-centered" ethic which has little regard for the quality of relationship between the persons involved. In addition, the procreative norm (if it can produce a child, it is somewhat justifiable) minimizes the injustice and suffering experienced by victims of sexual assault and condemns sexual activity which *by its nature* is not harmful or destructive, e.g., masturbation. The prevalence of this ethical teaching has contributed once again to the confusion and distortion of our understanding of sexual violence and sexual ethics.

Some criteria are needed to help judge the seriousness and the sinfulness of human behavior. But the criteria should be based on the degree to which a particular behavior causes damage or suffering to a person. Once the ethical question is reframed in this way, principles and criteria can be formulated to guide behavior and society's response to particular behaviors.

A second teaching from the Christian tradition is presented in the story of the Roman Catholic saint, Maria Goretti. At age 12, Maria Goretti was brutally attacked by a rapist. Although she successfully prevented herself from being raped, her attacker stabbed her to death. As she died, she forgave her murderer. The church's teaching derived from this event is conveyed in the tone and content of these passages from the homily delivered by Pope Pius XII at the canonization of St. Maria Goretti.

> Saint Maria was born of a poor family in Italy in 1890. Near Nettuno she spent a difficult childhood assisting her mother in domestic duties. She was of a pious nature and often at prayer. In 1902 she was stabbed to death, preferring to die rather than be raped.
>
> It is well known how this young girl had to face a bitter struggle with no way to defend herself. Without warning a vicious stranger burst upon her, bent on raping her and destroying her childlike purity. In that moment of crisis, she could have spoken to her Redeemer in the words of that classic, *The Imitation of Christ:* "Though tested and plagued by a host of misfortunes, I have no fear so long as your grace is with me. It is my strength, stronger than any adversary; it helps me and gives me guidance." With splendid courage she surrendered herself to God and his grace and so gave her life to protect her virginity.
>
> From Maria's story carefree children and young people with their zest for life can learn not to be led astray by attractive pleasures which are not only ephemeral and empty but also sinful. Instead they can fix their sights on achieving Christian moral perfection, however difficult that course may prove. With determination and God's help all of us can attain that goal by persistent effort and prayer.
>
> Not all of us are expected to die a martyr's death, but we are all called to the pursuit of Christian virtue.[19]

The Pope seems to regard rape as "being led astray by attractive pleasures." The belief that rape is sexually pleasurable and that its victim is sinful emerges once again. According to this story, it is preferable that a girl die rather than commit the sin of "losing her virginity" because of the rape. The confusion of sexual activity with sexual violence is reflected in this teaching. The attempted rape is seen as a sexual approach rather than as a violent attack. Unfortunately, this story was used in some Catholic schools to teach young women about sexuality, thus perpetuating the confusion: Sexuality, young women learn, involves a violent aggressive attack by a stranger; a righteous woman is to protect herself from sexual contact at all costs, including her life.[20] The moral lessons abound:

1. Virginity must be preserved at all costs, even death, because any sexual contact outside of marriage is sinful and the female's chaste property value must be maintained.
2. Women should actively resist male sexual aggression outside of marriage because it is sexual and therefore sinful.
3. It is the woman's responsibility to prevent sexual contact outside of marriage, violent or otherwise.

Unfortunately, this story does not teach women to resist male sexual aggression *for the right reasons,* i.e., because it is violent and aggressive and women have a right to maintain their bodily integrity. The figure of St. Maria Goretti presented by the church is one of the more blatant examples of a confused and distorted view of sexual violence and sexuality, and a source of the view that women have no value except as sexual property.

Contemporary Christian ethicists who do address sexual violence at all do so in a cursory manner. Here we often find a combination of constructive ethical insight and traditional ethical confusion. For example, in an article on sexual ethics, John T. Noonan, Jr., describes rape as

> the most universally abhorred sexual act; . . . it inflicts fear, bodily harm, and psychological trauma; . . . it creates the possibility of conception; . . . it invades the victim's privacy; . . . it expresses hatred. . . . It is the

touching of the genital zone accompanied by animosity, threat and trauma which makes rape repulsive.[21]

Even though he identifies it as an abhorrent *sexual* act rather than a *violent* act, he accurately describes the violation.

In *Embodiment* by James Nelson, one of the most useful books recently written on Christian sexual ethics, the author cites rape as a social justice issue and as a crime of "violence used to keep woman 'in their place.'" This is a valuable insight but beyond this, his treatment of rape is minimal.[22]

Like many traditional legal definitions, *Baker's Dictionary of Christian Ethics* defines rape as "a man's unlawful carnal knowledge of a woman, without her consent, by resort to force or fraud."[23] This definition emphasizes the important issues of consent and force, but adds that "corroboration by evidence other than the woman's testimony"[24] is required. A doubt remains as to a woman's trustworthiness. It also is interesting to note that this definition limits rape to male-female assault and does not recognize same-gender rape.

The Dictionary of Moral Theology, a Roman Catholic resource, emphasizes the violent nature of rape: "In the terminology of modern theologians, *rape* is a violent sexual relation . . . violence is understood not only as a physical but moral force (serious threats, deception)."[25] Added to this definition is the injustice of the "violation of the right of a woman to use her generative faculty according to her own choice."[26] But then it goes on to say that the rape of a virgin is a greater injustice because "virginity is a good of greatest value, distinct from the right that she has to the use of her own body according to her free choice."[27] Here the concern for sexual chastity overrides the principle of women's right to bodily integrity and autonomy. This concern is further emphasized: "In a case of violence, the woman is obliged to use all the means at her command to avoid *the sexual act* [emphasis added], short of exposing herself to the danger of death, or to other grave harm . . ."[28] This is one step short of the example

St. Maria Goretti gave the world. Finally, the ethical concern expressed here focuses on the maintenance of a woman's sexual chastity, which, at its core, is a concern for male property rights.[29]

> The unjust aggressor is obliged to make reparation of all damages due to his crime. In particular, he must enable the woman to contract marriage in the same manner as if she had never been violated, *even by marrying her himself*, [emphasis added] provided that all other conditions are favorable. . . . *Often the best form of reparation is marriage*, [emphasis added] if it can be properly arranged and offers a reasonable prospect of success.[30]

Published in 1962, *The Dictionary of Moral Theology* echoes Deuteronomy with its suggestion that a rape victim *marry* her rapist, and that such a marriage would make reparation *to her* for the crime![31]

In the *Biblical View of Sex and Marriage*, Otto Piper goes to the extreme of traditional interpretation and describes rape (along with masturbation) as that which results "when a normal satisfaction of the sexual desire is impossible."[32] He regards insatiable sexual need as the source of sexual violence and "never a conscious volition."[33] If never a conscious volition, then, we can conclude, rape is nothing that a rapist can be held accountable for.

In contemporary Christian ethical discussion, even less attention is given to incest than to rape. The primary concerns expressed are the potential for hereditary defects in children of an incestuous union[34] (although the scientific basis for this genetic concern is questionable), the impact of incest on the parents' relationship, and the need to maintain the "natural order of procreation."[35] These sources of contemporary ethical discussion make no reference to incestuous abuse being destructive to children or to it being a violation of the parent-child relationship.

Unlike *Baker's Dictionary* and the *Dictionary of Moral Theology*, Noonan does raise the ethical issues posed by comparing rape and incest. In his discussion, however, there is a mixture of accuracy and inaccuracy which limits its usefulness.

> Except where it merges with actual rape, incest is not necessarily attended by fear or bodily injury. In the paradigm case of father and pubescent daughter, it is typically attended by trauma for the child. It creates the possibility of a conception without responsible parents. It does not invade the child's privacy without her consent. It does not express hatred. It does distort the relation of a father to a daughter. It does involve a betrayal of the child's trust. The infliction of the trauma, the risking of a pregnancy, the distortion of the parental role, and the betrayal of trust are injuries to the individual and to society.[36]

There is often fear and can be bodily injury even without penetration. In fact, the typical case is father and a three- to six-year-old daughter when the abuse begins. There is definitely trauma for the child. The possibility of enforced conception is very real and must be addressed by the Church. He describes the damage and yet suggests that there is no invasion of privacy which is the basis for that damage done. While the incestuous abuse may not express hatred, it expresses a total disregard for the well-being of the child. Noonan accurately sums up the nature of the injury and its consequences. But he erroneously believes that the incest taboo is functioning to prevent incest.[37] Again there is minimal understanding of the ethical questions of consent, power, and powerlessness, and the protection of children.

Despite lip service to the contrary, it appears that contemporary Christian teaching, like traditional teaching, views sexual violence as either a sexual impropriety or a violation of male property rights. The occasional exceptions to this view are too few and too superficial to significantly challenge the dominant position of both Scripture and tradition.

The Christian tradition itself offers even less than the Scripture in providing clarity and direction for an ethical perspective on sexual violence. Too often the teachings of the tradition confuse sexual activity with sexual violence. In doing so, they focus on the sexual rather than on the violent aspect of sexual violence; they blame the victim; and they fail to hold the offender accountable. There is virtually no mention of the victim of sexual assault as the one who is offended directly. The context of justice is almost never put forth. Restitution *for the victim* is never mentioned. While there is some concern in Scripture for the impact of sexual violence on the whole community, the implications of this are never drawn. The tradition treats sexual assault as an embarrassing individual experience rather than as a cause for community outrage. Moreover, the traditional teachings contribute to the negative, ill-informed, and contradictory attitudes about female sexuality and homosexuality.

Traditional Christian Sexual Ethics

As we presented an overview of the Abuse Prevention Materials for Teenagers to parents and youth advisors in a local church, the final question from one of the adults was, "All I want to know is, are you going to tell them what is right and wrong?" The answer to his question was, "Yes, we are going to tell them that responsible, non-abusive sexual activity is right and that sexual abuse and exploitation is wrong."

While the absence of ethical and theological attention to sexual violence has been detrimental to the daily life of the Christian community, it is most keenly felt in the area of Christian sexual ethics. Traditional Christian sexual ethics have both suffered from and contributed to the confusion of responsible sexual activity with sexual violence and abuse. In addition, the concern of traditional Christian sexual ethics has been with the *form* rather than the *substance* of sexual relationships. The ethical question has been who was doing what with whom and when, or as James Nelson so aptly puts it, the question of "the right organ in the right orifice with the right person."[38] Little attention has been given to the context of power, consent, and choice regarding what happens to one's bodily self in a sexual relationship. This concern with form over substance in sexual relationships has meant that the confusion between sexual activity and sexual violence which dominates this society has gone unchallenged by Christian sexual ethics. A critical understanding of the ways in which traditional Christian ethical questions have been misplaced will make a reformation in Christian sexual ethics possible.

In traditional Christian sexual ethics the issues have focused on the form or type of sexual contact between persons. Consider how the following ethical questions are stated:

- Should persons engage in sexual activity before marriage?
- Should persons of the same gender engage in sexual activity?
- Should persons engage in any nonprocreative sexual activity?
- Should a person engage in extramarital activity?
- Should older persons engage in sexual activity?
- Should a person engage in masturbation?

All of these questions focus on the who, what, where, when, and why of sexual activity. None of them considers the substance of the sexual interaction, for example, the quality of the relationship, including the presence or absence of consent and the distribution of power.

While some of the questions do require ethical discussion concerning the form of relationships (who, what, when, where, and why), that discussion needs to be directed primarily toward the consideration of commitment and relationship.[39] Thus, for example, the question of extramarital (or extracommitment) sexual activity is more accurately a question of extracommitment intimacy which may or may not be sexual. The question could be stated thus: Is it ethically right and good to engage in intimate activity (sexual, emotional, etc.) outside of one's primary committed relationship? The answer to this question depends on the terms of the primary commitment, the experience of the partners, and the willingness to take the advice of others who may say that it is emotionally impractical to engage in extracommitment intimacy.

Using this broader framework, the issue is not whether it is categorically wrong to engage in extracommitment sexual activity. The ethical concern has to do with the impact of such activity on a marriage or commitment. While it is morally wrong to violate such a commitment, sexual activity may or may not cause this violation. Thus in considering extracommitment activity, it is not the sexual nature of the activity *per se* that requires ethical reflection but the intimate nature of the activity and its impact on the relationship. Does intimate activity with another person outside of a committed relationship violate that commitment? Does it diminish one's ability to fulfill one's responsibilities to one's partner? While the sexual nature of the activity is significant because it represents the potential for greater intimacy, it is not the central issue. The purpose here is not to discuss the issue of extracommitment sexual activity in depth; however, it does provide an example of a way in which those questions traditionally regarded as issues of sexual ethics can be restated and reexamined.

The question of whether persons should engage in sexual activity before marriage is another example of misplaced ethical focus. The traditional *rule* which said categorically that sexual activity before marriage was wrong implied that sexual activity in marriage was right; no other criteria need be applied.[40] The primary consideration was *when* sexual activity took place. It gave little consideration to the substance or quality of the sexual interaction after marriage. Using this view, it would be wrong for a man to engage in coercive sexual activity with a woman before they were married, and acceptable for him to engage in exactly the same coercive sexual activity after they were married. This is the ethical stance which makes it possible to suggest that there is no such thing as marital rape because marriage assures the husband any form of sexual access to his wife at any time. The question of the substance and quality of the sexual interaction, the presence of consent, etc. is never raised.

Again, ethical reflection on sexual activity before, during, or after marriage or commitment needs to be reframed. The primary considerations relevant to sexual activity have to do with choice, equal regard for the needs of the other, consent, mutuality, and respect. Does the sexual activity in which one engages in a relationship take these concerns into account? Does this activity enhance and sustain one's commitment to a partner? The issue is not whether sexual activity before marriage or commitment is categorically wrong, but rather, what is the quality and substance of that activity (should the couple *choose* it)? How does it affect their relationship before and after commitment? How does it affect their relationship with God? Two persons may very well decide not to engage in sexual activity prior to a commitment between them based on this reexamination of the issues. But their reasons for doing so will be grounded in their shared values and mutual decision-making process rather than based on an arbitrary, categorical rule. This will prepare them for continuing ethical reflection concerning their sexual activities after the commitment is made.

The concern as to whether or not two persons of the same gender should engage in sexual activity is another example of misplaced ethical concern. At different points in the history of the Christian tradition the church has used misinterpretations of Scripture and drawn on prevailing cultural attitudes to condemn same-gender sexual activity. Again the implication is that *any* sexual contact between persons of the same gender is wrong. The concern here is the questions of *who* is involved in sexual activity. Stated in this way, the question of quality of relationship or sexual interaction is never raised. Using this approach, coercive or even violent sexual contact between persons of the opposite gender may be excused while consenting, responsible sexual activity with the same gender is readily condemned.

To suggest that same-gender sexual activity is categorically wrong cuts short the process of ethical reflection and may well limit the possibility for the formation of responsible, committed relationships. In restating the ethical concerns related to same-gender sexual activity, the ethical norms or expectations should focus on the quality of the sexual relationship regardless of gender.

For the most part, sexual ethics have been limited to categorical regulations because of an overriding concern with a procreative norm for sexual ethics. The emphasis on this norm for Christian sexual ethics is rooted in the value the Hebrews placed on reproduction in order to sustain a small, struggling population. To a large degree, sexual activity which produced children was encouraged and that which did not was discouraged. Thus polygamy was common; homosexuality and coitus interruptus were discouraged. Although the Biblical record does not discuss masturbation as such, the historic position of both the Jewish and Christian communities has condemned it because it is seen as nonprocreative activity. In addition, the influence of Stoic philosophy on the Christian procreative norm is significant. Stoics believed that sexual desire was irrational and that sexual activity could only be justified if it served a rational purpose like procreation.[41] The position of the Roman Catholic Church today remains that sexual activity should take place only in the context of marriage and preferably for purposes of procreation. However, the approval of the rhythm method by Pope Pius XI in 1930 has made nonprocreative (as distinguished from anti-procreative) sexual activity by Catholics legitimate in the eyes of the Church.[42] Most Protestant groups have broadened their understanding of acceptable sexual activity beyond a procreative norm to include the use of artificial birth control methods as a means of responsible stewardship. Still the procreative norm remains a significant influence in determining what is regarded as "natural" and "unnatural" in sexual activity. The "natural/unnatural" criteria frequently determine what is regarded as morally right or wrong. (See "The Christian Tradition on Sexual Violence.") For example, same-gender sexual contact is seen as morally wrong because it is unnatural; it is unnatural because it is not procreative. Thus, the influence of the procreative norm remains a part of the dominant cultural and religious attitudes even now.

The tendencies of traditional sexual ethics to be "act-centered," that is, focusing on form, and using the procreative norm as a primary criterion, have meant that little attention has been given to the issues of consent and power in sexual relationships. Hence, traditional sexual ethics have often missed the mark by providing a list of "thou shalt nots" and utilizing guilt as a means to encourage conformity to the rules of the Church rather than teaching persons how to make ethical choices. To make responsible ethical choices in the area of sexuality requires information, a willingness to communicate and negotiate, a respect for the other's choices, a sense of self-worth, and a sense of one's own power to consent or withhold consent. The Church has not adequately prepared people to engage in ethical decisionmaking. Instead it has sought to control people's sexual behavior through fear, guilt, and regulation.

It is far simpler to leave the discussion of ethical sexual behavior at the level of category and regulation than to focus ethical discourse on substance and quality. To do this means questioning some of the most basic assumptions in our culture about men, women, and sexuality. Perhaps this is one reason that most Christian sexual ethics seem obsessed with the who, what, where, when, and why approach to sexuality. The implications of a deeper ethical reflection are complex and often disquieting. However, our unwillingness to reframe the ethical questions surrounding sexuality is a detriment to our lives and to the community and perpetuates the distortion of human sexuality.

This critical review of scriptural and traditionally-oriented contemporary sources leads to the conclusion that Scripture and Christian tradition are inadequate for helping to address sexual violence as an ethical issue. Thus, it is clear that in order to engage constructively in ethical discourse, we must be willing to discard that material which is ill-informed and perpetuates confusion, and draw more deeply on our faith and experience.

Using these resources, we must then reframe the ethical questions presented by sexual violence, clarifying the confusion between sexual activity and sexual violence, and asking what is the real violation which takes place when a person is raped or sexually abused. We must name the unmentionable sin. Then we must struggle with the demands which justice makes in response to the sin of sexual violence. Finally, we must consider the implications for contemporary Christian sexual ethics.

Naming the Unmentionable Sin

The sin of sexual violence has gone largely unmentioned for centuries. The question of what is wrong about sexual violence or what is the sin of sexual violence has never been adequately addressed in Christian ethics. Why is it wrong to rape someone or to molest a child? The answer which to some may seem self-evident has, in fact, remained largely elusive. When mentioned at all, the understanding of the sin of sexual violence has been distorted, used to condemn victims as sinful, defined as an offense against male property rights, or equated with adultery by interpreting sexual violence as "sexual activity outside of marriage."

Consequently, naming the sin of sexual violence requires redefining "sin" and reframing the sin of sexual violence as an ethical issue. The focus of accountability which has traditionally been misplaced needs correction. In describing the sinful nature of sexual violence, the norm of right relation between persons needs to be posited in order to understand the violation of this norm which sexual violence represents. Finally, given this understanding of the sin of sexual violence, what is a just response to this sin? The remainder of this chapter will name the unmentionable sin and suggest a just response within a Christian ethical framework.

WHOSE SIN IS THIS?

Most often the sin of sexual violence has been attributed to the victim rather than to the offender. Arlene Swidler refutes this in an article published in *U.S. Catholic* titled "It's No Sin to Be Raped." She refers to a news story about a Roman Catholic priest who said that it was "better for girls to die than to submit to rape."[43] Because of this attitude (which is reinforced by the story of St. Maria Goretti) and others which place responsibility for rape on its victims, many Christians hold the opinion that the sin of sexual violence is the victim's, not the rapist's.

The belief that the rape victim is sinful is manifest in two ways. The first view combines superstition (the irrational belief that two isolated experiences are causally related) with a belief in a punitive God. The victimization itself is seen as punishment for previous sin. Any prior indiscretion, violation of a religious commandment or law, or act of meanness becomes the cause for the punishment. For example, a woman who was a rape victim reasoned that her rape was God's punishment because she masturbated when she was a teenager.

The second belief comes from the idea that "good women

do not get raped." This is a common attitude and is often reflected in questions directed at the victim: "What were you wearing? Where were you going? What were you doing that caused the attack?" Underlying these questions is the idea that if she had been behaving in a proper, righteous manner, she would not have been assaulted.[44] The fact that she was raped is evidence to the contrary. More specifically, if she were "a good Christian woman," God would have protected her from the attack. Her victimization becomes a sign of *her* sinfulness.

This overriding concern with the possible sinfulness of the victim was an issue discussed at length by Augustine in *The City of God*. Initially Augustine states clearly that a victim of violence or lust, i.e., sexual violence, is not culpable. (It is ironic that Augustine refers to only males in his discussion of victims of lust.):

> . . . it is the exercise of the consecrated will that makes the body holy. If that will remain unshaken and firm, whatever anyone else does to or with the body, the sufferer incurs no fault, so long as he could not escape the assault without committing some offence of his own. Now what can be done against the body of another includes not only violence but lust. Whatever belongs to the latter category does not destroy the chastity that is firmly held by the constant mind.[45]

Since chastity is a state of mind, it cannot be taken away by a rapist. However, then Augustine immediately cautions that perhaps the victim really consented: "Yet the assault inflicts shame upon the sufferer from belief that the will may have consented to the deed, since it could probably not be effected at all without some yielding to fleshly pleasure."[46]

This passage reflects that commonly held suspicion that the rape victim really did want to be raped; as the saying goes, "you cannot thread a moving needle." If a woman had actively resisted, rape would have been impossible. The victim is further blamed by circular reasoning. Feelings of shame or embarrassment in the victim are regarded by others as signs that the victim consented and enjoyed the illicit sexual act for which she now feels ashamed. The fact is that these feelings result from the blame society placed on the victim. In Augustine's final analysis, the fact that the rape took place at all indicates that the victim was somehow responsible. He writes: "No one, however modest and superior, has it in his power to decide what may be done to his body, only what his mind will accept or refuse."[47] That is to say that no one finally can decide what happens to their physical body because everyone is vulnerable to physical attack; a person can only decide whether to accept or refuse to accept what is done physically to her/him. While Augustine is correct in describing a person's lack of power in many cases to determine bodily integrity, he unfortunately does not affirm that one under any circumstance has the *right* "to decide what may be done to his body." (See Chapter 4, "Consensual Sex and a New Sexual Ethic.")

Both society and the church have been hesitant, if not unwilling, to place responsibility for acts of sexual abuse and assault on the offender. Naming the sin accurately allows us to place the responsibility where it belongs. It is the offender's sin. It is a sin against God, the offender, the victim, and the community with serious ramifications for all.

REDEFINING "SIN" AND "GOD" AND CLAIMING BOTH

The use of the word "sin" to describe sexual violence may be initially unfamiliar or misleading for some readers. Too often "sin" is based on an ethical system which emphasizes rules and regulations about specific acts. It often describes the focus of pietistic and moralistic religious beliefs; it may be the bedrock of condemnation and judgment. This is not the concept of "sin" used here.

"Sin" is alienation, brokenness, and estrangement. It is a

dimension of human experience which describes one's estrangement from self, others, and God. This estrangement is
contrary to the created order and contradicts God's intention
for our lives. Persons are created in God's image and created
to be in relationship. To know oneself and to be oneself is to
be in relationship with others and with God.[48] Affirmation of
our relational existence is one of the insights of Jewish and
Christian theology.[49] Sin is the rupture of relationship and
may be experienced psychologically, physically, spiritually,
and socially. All persons know estrangement, brokenness,
and alienation at some time in their lives. Salvation (or redemption) overcomes sin and brings healing and restoration
of relationship.[50] Moments of healing, wholeness, and new
life are moments of grace. "The experience of the new life is a
relational reality in which the miraculous and everyday stuff
of life are interwoven. The incarnation of God, the divine
presence in and through human flesh, is always a miracle."[51]
Likewise this experience of grace is accessible to every person
who seeks to overcome estrangement and brokenness. God is
the source of grace.

Like the concept of "sin," the concept of "God" is
troublesome for some and is open to misinterpretation and
misuse. God can now be understood to be that dimension of
divine presence which is the source of all life (God the
Creator), offers persons grace and reconciliation (God the Redeemer), and dwells in and among all persons always (God the
Sustainer). This loosely Trinitarian understanding of God emphasizes the God-within and seeks to de-emphasize the God-
over-there. It is a God who seeks justice, not revenge. It is a
God who stands with the oppressed and over against the op-
pressor. It is a God who suffers with the suffering of people.
This understanding of God which has developed out of liberation and feminist theologies is the understanding referred to
here by the use of the word "God."

Within the broad and somewhat abstract notion of sin as a

dimension of human experience, sins are the individual or collective acts of those who are estranged and broken, acts which bring suffering to others. The sinful person strikes out at others in hostility and anger, denying the demands of relationship and violating the personhood of others by treating them as objects or by intentionally inflicting injury. The wages of sin are violence, and the consequences are suffering for all involved.

Redemption is the healing of this brokenness, which may lead to the renewal of the relationship with God, self, and others. In order for this to take place sins must be acknowledged and repented; change must be apparent and genuine; and restitution must be made for the suffering caused. When these things are done, a context of justice is created and forgiveness can follow. Only then can reconciliation become a possibility.

THE NORM OF RIGHT RELATIONSHIP

If persons are created by God to be in relationship, then what is the *norm of right relationship?* What is necessary in a relationship in order that it be affirming of persons and pleasing to God? A description of right relationship begins within the context of love and justice. The New Testament's concept of love is *agape*, a love that moves persons to seek union with others (friends, acquaintances, coworkers, partners, family members, and even strangers) and God. The concept of justice requires a relationship which includes mutuality, equality, shared power, trust, choice, responsibility, and respect for bodily integrity.[52] These aspects of a relationship are prerequisites for a just interaction which seeks equal regard for the welfare of self and others.

In evaluating a relationship with another person to determine if it has the qualities of right relation, i.e., is grounded in love and justice, one might consider the following:

- Do I share the power equally in this relationship?
- Do I respect the wishes of the other person and my own regarding intimacy and physical or sexual contact?
- Do I trust that the other person will not betray or intentionally injure me?
- Do I freely and with full knowledge choose to interact with this person?
- Does the other person freely and with full knowledge choose to interact with me?

If these questions can be answered affirmatively, then persons can assume that the possibility of right relationship exists between them.

Some relationships, by nature of the roles of the two persons involved, do not include all of the qualities described here. Specifically, this is the case when the roles in the relationship create an imbalance of power between the two persons. The relationship between counselor and client, parent and child, teacher and student, pastor and parishioner, and doctor and patient all represent relationships where one person has greater power than the other. The imbalance of power may be a function of role, difference in age, gender, physical size and strength, etc. Overall it is the responsibility of the person with the greater power and authority to avoid misusing the power to take advantage of the vulnerability of the less powerful person. The person in the authority role is expected to meet the needs of the other person for support, education, guidance, counsel, information, and to safeguard the other's welfare. The person in the authority role should not expect to have his/her primary needs met in a parental or professional relationship. Avoiding this expectation requires clearly understanding and adhering to one's role and not confusing this relationship with a peer relationship between equals. In addition, the community has a responsibility through statutes, ethics codes of professional organizations, or denominations, etc., to provide checks and balances for parental or professional accountability. The norm of right relationship is based on love and justice and ordinarily requires equal power between persons. When there is a legitimate reason for the absence of equal power, as in a professional relationship or a familial relationship between adults and children, then right relationship is possible only if the less powerful person is protected from exploitation and abuse by the more powerful person. At such time that an unequal relationship is ended and an equal relationship takes its place, this provision is no longer a priority. This would be the case when a child reaches adulthood and a parent gives up the authority role in order to build a new, equal relationship. This would also be possible when therapy is terminated between counselor and client, at which time, if both persons choose, a relationship between equals might be established.

VIOLATION OF RIGHT RELATION IS SIN

Given this context for right relations between persons, sin is the violation of right relation which results in alienation, brokenness, and mistrust between the two people and suffering for the one violated. The violation of right relation is the essence of injustice or, as Carter Heyward suggests, evil:

> Where there is no moral act of love, no justice, there is an evil situation. *Evil is an act*, not a metaphysical principle or a passive absence of good. Evil is the act of un-love or in-justice. It is the doing of moral wrong, specifically of breaking the relational bond between and among ourselves in such a way that one, both, or many parties are disempowered to grow, love, and/or live.[53]

Specifically, any form of sexual coercion or violence inflicted on another is a violation of right relation and so is unjust, evil, and sinful. It violates a person's bodily integrity, denies that person self-determination and choice, causes physical and psychological injury, creates fear, may be life-threatening, destroys the possibility of trust (especially if there was a trusting relationship prior to the assault, e.g., with a friend or family member), takes advantage of vulnerability (weakness, disability, youth, personal crisis, or subordinate position), carries for women the possibility of enforced pregnancy, distorts and misuses sexuality to harm another person, and precludes the possibility of right relationship. In short, sexual violence creates victims. In this situation, the intent of the offender is not the issue. The consequence of injury to the victim even when unintended or inadvertent[54] is what defines the act as one of violation and violence. The creation of a victim also creates a victimizer. The possibility of right relationship between the two is nonexistent.

Central to the concept of the violation of right relation which sexual violence represents is the violation of bodily integrity. In matters of physical and sexual contact, the right to bodily integrity is the right to establish physical boundaries and to choose what is done to one's body and by one's body. Exercising choice means giving or withholding consent to different forms of sexual contact or activity. This choice is meaningful only if a person has sufficient information upon which to base a choice and sufficient power by which to have that choice respected by others. Without these conditions, there is no real alternative but to submit to the demands of the other person. For example, a 4-year-old does not know that fathers are not supposed to have sexual contact with their children; a 35-year-old retarded woman has minimal information about sexuality and is totally dependent on her guardian; a 45-year-old wife has full knowledge but is overpowered by the sexual demands of her husband and economically dependent upon him. For all of these persons, meaningful choice is denied. Bodily integrity is violated whenever any form of coercion or violence prevents persons from exercising choice in regard to their physical or sexual selves.

In any situation of sexual coercion or violence, the conditions for right relation are absent. The offender's action prevents right relation or destroys it if it had been present prior to his action. Violation of right relation is the sin of sexual violence.

Sexual violence is a sin against the victim. It is sinful, not because of its sexual nature *per se,* but because it is an exploitative and abusive violation of the victim's bodily integrity. It denies and violates the personhood of the victim. In terms of a theology of creation, in which we affirm persons as created in God's own image, acts of sexual violence are blasphemous; they deny the sacredness of the other person. The victim is either used as an object or harm is intentionally inflicted upon her/him. The assault humiliates, dominates, degrades, overpowers, and violates a person through the most vulnerable dimension of self, the sexual self. Often the victim feels abandoned by God, denying that resource when it is most needed.

From the offender's perspective, his violation of the bodily integrity of another is an obvious infraction of the commandment to love one's neighbor as oneself (Mark 12: 31), i.e., to treat other people with equal regard for their welfare, seeking a just and right relationship. The choice of the offender to victimize the other is to choose that which is life-denying rather than life-affirming, both for the victim and for himself. "I have set before you life and death, blessing and curse; therefore, choose life . . ." (Deuteronomy 30: 19), i.e., choose that which builds up and affirms life in each person rather than that which diminishes life.

Sexual violence for the offender is a sin against the self. It is a denial of one's selfhood, a destruction of relationship with another, and a distortion of one's own sexuality. Not only is the sex offender committing sinful acts, he is "living in a state of sin," alienated and separated from self and from God. His alienation contributes to his acts of violence against others. The source of his alienation may well be his own victimization as a child or teenager. Many offenders were abused or exploited, physically or sexually, as children. (See Chapter 9,

"Responding to Sex Offenders.") This childhood victimization resulted in a negative self-image, isolation, alienation, anger, and hostility.[55] Yet comprehending the sources of the offender's problem (spiritual, psychological, social) in no way excuses his behavior. He is still to be held accountable for his sinful acts against others.

Sexual violence is a sin against the community. The Old Testament references to rape rightly relate the offense to the disruption of community life.[56] They describe the upset of male property arrangements which resulted from sexual violence. But reinterpreted from the perspective of the victims, we can better understand the disruption of the community to mean the fear, mistrust, and limitations which sexual violence imposes on all members of the community. The Old Testament words describe the havoc, folly,[57] and emptiness which resulted from sexual assault. A picture emerges of a hostile, alien environment which diminishes the possibility of meaningful relationships within the community, particularly between women and men. From a Christian perspective, the sin of sexual violence is also a sin against the community of faith as a whole. Because through baptism, all Christians are joined together as one body, whenever any one of its members is violated or injured, the whole body suffers from the sin.

Finally, sexual violence is a sin against God because it is the violation of God's most sacred creation, a human being. Sexual violence is also a misuse and distortion of a gift from God. Sexuality was given by God as a blessing to strengthen and build up human relationships and community. It is a celebration of our incarnate being. Sexual violence is antithetical to the intention of sexuality. It is the misuse and abuse of that which was given for good; it destroys relationships rather than enhances them. One who commits acts of sexual violence does so out of a deep alienation from God and self. Having denied or separated oneself from God, the sex offender has little sense of relationship with God who is the source of his being.

The sin of sexual violence is multidimensional.

- It is bodily sin: a violation of the bodily integrity of another person.
- It is a relational sin: a violation of trust in a relationship which destroys the possibility of relationship between people.
- It is a social sin: It thrives in an environment of sexism which sustains subordinate/dominant relationships and encourages or silently condones individual acts of sexual violence, creating a hostile environment particularly for women and children.
- It is a sexual sin: It is not a sin *because* it is sexual; rather sexual violence is the distortion and misuse of sexuality, and thus a sin against sexuality.

The sin of sexual violence brings suffering for everyone and diminishes our life together. This cycle of suffering can and must be broken.

THE JUST RESPONSE TO THE SIN OF SEXUAL VIOLENCE

In the face of this sin, what is the just response? What is necessary to right the relation which is broken by this sin?

The first response of justice to the sins of sexual violence is *righteous anger*. When Jesus saw that the moneylenders were misusing the Temple, he forcefully cleared them out (John 2: 14–17). His righteous anger moved him to act in the face of the violation of the temple and he cast out the offenders. His action was not vengeful; rather he intervened to stop the abuse. The image of Jesus and the Temple is even more powerful if we understand the body to be a temple of the Holy Spirit (John 2: 21 and I Corinthians 6: 12–20). Surely the violation of persons and relationships deserves no less a response.

The second response of justice is *compassion for the victims*. Binding up the wounds, the injured bodies and spirits of the victims, is the critical need. Like the Good Samaritan, the Church is called to get involved, expend resources, and take the risk of helping the victims of sexual violence.

The third response of justice is *advocacy for the victim*. To be a victim is to be made temporarily powerless in the face of not only the offender but also the community. This makes it difficult for a victim to deal immediately with the necessary medical and legal systems. Victims often need someone to stand by them as they seek help from the community.

The fourth response of justice is *holding the offender legally and spiritually accountable* for his/her sin against the victim and the community. However, for the offender to be accountable, he/she must first acknowledge what he/she did and the suffering that the action caused both the victim and the community. Then he/she must repent. One sign of true repentance is a change in the offender, i.e., a desire to do whatever it takes to change his/her aggressive and destructive behavior. (See Chapter 9, "Responding to Sex Offenders.") Another act of repentance is restitution. Restitution clearly acknowledges the offender's responsibility for the sin as well as the need to make right the injuries done to the victim. Although material or financial means are seldom adequate to restore the victim's complete well-being, payments can assist with medical costs. Restitution payments to a rape crisis center or victims' compensation program contributes to services made necessary by the offender's actions. In this way, the offender makes restitution to the community as well. Even if an offender does not repent or make restitution, the community can still hold him/her accountable by due process of law and protect itself by incarcerating him/her.

The response of justice to the offender who has repented through rehabilitation and restitution is *understanding and forgiveness*. Forgiveness on the part of the victim is a complex pastoral issue which is discussed in more detail in Part 2 (see Chapter 10, "Religious Concerns and Pastoral Issues"). However, forgiveness, i.e., a willingness on the part of the community to allow the offender to begin anew, is the final stage of justice-making which can lead ultimately to the offender's reconciliation with himself/herself and the community. Such forgiveness can only follow the offender's acknowledgment of the offense and its impact and his/her repentance. Otherwise, forgiveness is an empty gesture. This is not a time for cheap grace or premature reconciliation. While Christians believe in God's mercy and forgiveness, we also believe that such forgiveness comes to those who are *truly repentant* of their sin. It does not come to those who seek quick and easy absolution or to those who subtly manipulate the concerns of the victim and the community to serve their own self-interest and to avoid responsibility. Furthermore, forgiveness should not be used by the community as a panacea for its discomfort in having to deal with sexual violence in the first place. Forgiveness by the community requires a clear confrontation and acknowledgment that one within it has been wronged by another and that the offender has to take steps to rectify that wrong. Justice is not served by a wishy-washy response that simply overlooks the offense with the reminder that we all have clay feet and make mistakes sometimes. Acts of sexual abuse or violence are serious and have a devastating impact on the victim, her/his family, and the fabric of the community. Justice requires that the community deal with these acts with appropriate seriousness.[58]

While the offense of sexual violence is serious, and while the community must respond in order to carry out justice and protect its members, retribution is *not* a just response to the offender, i.e. capital punishment for sexual assault, long-term imprisonment without treatment, or complete ostracism. All of these further the offender's brokenness. The ends of justice and reconciliation are never served by retribution. The cycle of violence is never broken.

The fifth response of justice is *prevention*. Society needs to take responsibility for the ways in which it serves to sustain an environment that seldom challenges and often encourages sexual violence. Justice requires that everything possible be done to prevent sexual violence from ever claiming another victim. This means changes in many areas of persons' collective and individual lives in order to address the roots (e.g., sexism, child abuse, sexual ethics, economics) and not merely the symptoms of sexual violence. (See Chapter 12, "Strategies for Action.")

Sexual violence occurs in contemporary society in which racism is an endemic and virulent social problem. Any discussion of a just response to sexual violence must include a discussion of racism and sexual violence. Racism affects society's view of sexual violence, and it consequently shapes society's response to victims and offenders. Racism is manifest in a number of attitudes, beliefs, and practices related to sexual violence.

Most sexual assault occurs *within* racial groups;[59] however, it's commonly believed among whites that white women are most likely to be raped by men of color. This belief has been taught to white women and has served to sustain suspicion and fear between whites and people of color. It has also distracted white women from realizing that their most likely assailant will be a white man.

Racism contributes to the minimization of sexual violence against women of color. Cultural attitudes which view women of color as being of less worth than white women and as "naturally sexually promiscuous" cause society not to respond to their victimization. Reports to police from women of color are too often regarded as false, or, if true, unimportant and undeserving of attention. If the offender is a white male, the assumption is that he can take what he wants. If the offender is a male of color, it's assumed that "that's the way those people behave normally." In either case, the experience of the woman of color who is raped is minimized. Although women of color are more frequently victims of rape[60] they are less likely to seek assistance through established resources like police, hospitals, or rape crisis lines. They avoid these institutions because of a history of insensitivity or neglect by these agencies in response to people of color. Women of color often find themselves in a position of being an easy target for rape and without recourse or support from established agencies and services.[61]

Racism also encourages the use of men of color as scapegoats. If the alleged offender is a man of color, authorities are likely to arrest any man of color whether or not he is the offender, to prosecute aggressively, and when convicted to sentence heavily. This is especially true if the victim is white. Alice Walker describes the context:

> Who knows what the black woman thinks of rape? Who has asked her? Who *cares*? Who has even properly acknowledged that *she* and not the white woman in this story is the most likely victim of rape? Whenever interracial rape is mentioned, a black woman's first thought is to protect the lives of her brothers, her father, her sons, her lover. A history of lynching has bred this reflex in her. I feel it as strongly as anyone.[62]

A double standard of justice persists in which a disproportionate number of men of color are arrested, convicted, and sentenced for sexual assaults of white women while white men who rape are less likely to be prosecuted at all. Capital punishment continues to be disproportionately employed as the sentence for a man of color who is convicted of raping a white woman.[63] Whenever an innocent man of color is convicted and sentenced, not only is a gross injustice committed but no progress is made in curbing sexual violence: A guilty rapist continues to rape while an innocent man pays a price.

The history of dealing with rape in the U.S. is filled with instances of racism. Since most rape laws until recently were property laws protecting the husband or father of the rape victim, it is no surprise that the legal system was most concerned with the protection of white men's property. Whenever the legal system could not be manipulated to this end, lynching was an available alternative. Lynching a man of color for supposedly assaulting a white woman served to terrorize the minority community and limit their activity to change unjust laws and practices. It also made clear to white women that they would be "protected" as long as they kept their place, i.e., did not question their status as property of husband or father, albeit prized possession. Unfortunately, some white women acting out of class and/or racial privilege falsely accused men of color of sexual assault. The most notable case of this was the Scottsboro Trial in the 1930s. Nine black men were falsely accused of rape by two white women at the insistence of a posse of white men who believed that rape had been committed. It took until 1951 to win the release of the last "Scottsboro Boy."

Because of this history, it is no surprise that many men and women of color initially responded with suspicion when white women began to organize against rape in 1970. Was this yet another way that whites would use to harass people of color in the U. S.? Unfortunately, some white women's naïveté and insensitivity to these concerns only confirmed these suspicions.[64] There have been serious difficulties within the anti-rape movement because of its inability to address issues of class and race.

Anyone who is genuinely concerned about confronting and preventing sexual violence must always evaluate their efforts in light of the ever-present reality of racism. Otherwise there is the risk of once again seeking to solve one problem only to exacerbate another. Thus, reform of the legal and corrections systems must go hand in hand with more effective arrest, conviction, and sentencing of offenders. Services to victims must provide for the different needs and perspectives of racial and ethnic groups.[65] Constant attention to institutional and individual racism will greatly increase the likelihood of developing a truly just response to sexual violence.[66]

Notes

1. This teaching has some validity as is reflected in the case of the Scottsboro Boys in the 1930s. Here two white women falsely accused a group of black men of rape. The innocent men were convicted and all served prison sentences.

2. We can assume that this matter would have been handled in later years according to the Deuteronomic laws rather than arbitrarily by the victim's brothers. The laws appear to have developed as a means of dealing with the violation of property which sexual assault represented.

3. Raymond E. Brown, S.S., Joseph A. Fitzmyer, S.J., Roland E. Murphy, O. Carm, *The Jerome Biblical Commentary* (Englewood Cliffs, N.J.: Prentice-Hall, 1969), p. 79.

4. The only exception to this is the son-father prohibition which is included because the father is obviously not the possession of the son.

5. In addition to the Levitical sources, Florence Rush suggests that there is evidence in the Talmudic writings of sexual license taken with young girls who were not close kin. "The Talmud held that a female child of 'three years and one day' could be betrothed by sexual intercourse with her father's permission. Intercourse with one younger was not a crime, but invalid. If a prospective groom would penetrate the child just once more after her third birthday, he could legitimately claim his promised bride." Florence Rush, *The Best Kept Secret* (Englewood Cliffs, N.J.: Prentice-Hall, 1980), p. 17. The practice of child rape in order to acquire a wife rests exclusively on the designation of female children as property who grow up to become wives. The property status never changes, only the owner. The only control over this practice of child rape was exercised by the girl's father who could withhold his permission for her to be raped. But he was unlikely to refuse an opportunity to have her designated to her husband at an early age.

6. "The laws focus mainly upon external threats to the man's authority, honor and property, though they may occasionally serve to define and protect his rights in relation to members of his own household." Phyllis Byrd, "Image of Women in the

Old Testament" in *Religion and Sexism* (New York: Simon & Schuster, 1974), p. 51.

7. This is the case for Protestant and Hebrew scriptures. Jerome's Latin translation includes three additional stories about Daniel translated into Latin from Greek, attributed to Theoditus. (Brown, Fitzmyer, and Murphy, p. 459.) But the emphasis here is on the use of the passage to encourage chastity and discourage sexual activity. Although included, it misinterprets the events and results in an anti-sexual message more than an anti-violence one.

8. Brown, Fitzmyer, and Murphy, p. 459.

9. *Encyclopedia of Bioethics*, S.V. "Sexual Ethics," by Margaret Farley (New York: Free Press, 1978), p. 1576.

10. "There are lusts of many kinds, but when the word is used simply without addition it would not occur to anyone that it mean anything but sexual emotion. This affects not only the whole body in an external sense, but also in an interior sense. It moves the whole man by a combined appetite of both body and mind. That is why it produces the greatest pleasure of which the body is capable, so that at the moment of consummation practically the whole watch and ward of reasoned thought is overwhelmed." Augustine, *City of God* (London: Oxford University Press, 1963), pp. 235–36. Unfortunately, Augustine regards this expression as "the greatest pleasure of which the body is capable," implying that male sexuality is dependent on "violent sexual appetite."

11. James Nelson also makes this distinction in his interpretation of Matthew 5:28: "And if lust is untamed, inordinate sexual desire which is not only the passion for *possession* of another but which also becomes, by its very centrality in the self, an expression of *idolatry*, then we are dealing here with something different from the usual erotic awareness expressed in sexual fantasy." James Nelson, *Embodiment* (Minneapolis, Mn.: Augsburg Publishing House, 1978), p. 162.

12. See Rosemary Radford Ruether, ed., *Religion and Sexism* (New York: Simon & Schuster, 1974).

13. *Encyclopedia of Witchcraft and Demonology*, S.V. "Malleus Maleficarum," Rossell Hope Robbins (New York: Crown Publishing, Inc., 1959), pp. 337–40.

14. *Malleus Maleficarum,* quoted in Rosemary Radford Ruether, *New Woman—New Earth* (New York: Seabury Press, 1978), pp. 97–98.

15. Rosemary Radford Ruether, *New Woman—New Earth* (New York: Seabury Press, 1978), p. 102.

16. Florence Rush, *The Best Kept Secret: Sexual Abuse of Children* (Englewood Cliffs, N.J.: Prentice-Hall, 1980), p. 39.

17. Anthony Kosnik et al., *Human Sexuality* (New York: Paulist Press, 1977), pp. 43–44.

18. *Ibid.,* p. 43.

19. *Celebrating the Saints* (New York: Pueblo Publishing Co., 1973), pp. 171–73.

20. These themes are echoed in the Susanna story discussed above. See Chapter 3, "Reframing the Ethical Questions."

21. John T. Noonan, "Genital Good," *Communio,* vol. VIII (Fall 1981), pp. 200–1.

22. James Nelson, *Embodiment* (Minneapolis, Mn.: Augsburg Publishing House, 1978), p. 262.

23. *Baker's Dictionary of Christian Ethics,* Carl F.H. Henry, ed. (Grand Rapids, Mi.: Baker Book House, 1973), p. 565.

24. *Ibid.*

25. *Dictionary of Moral Theology* (Westminister, Md.: Newman Press, 1962), p. 1017.

26. *Ibid.*

27. *Ibid.,* pp. 1017–18.

28. *Ibid.,* p. 1018.

29. In this we see the reflection of Aquinas who was most concerned about injury done to husband or father rather than to the rape victim herself. Oscar E. Feucht et al., *Sex and the Church* (St. Louis, Mo.: Concordia Publishing House, 1961), p. 70.

30. *Dictionary of Moral Theology,* p. 1018.

31. This text is the only one cited here which addresses the question of what happens if a woman does conceive from rape: "It is a disputed question whether, immediately following intercourse, the woman may use positive means to prevent conception or must let nature take its course." *Dictionary of Moral Theology,* p. 1018. While moral theologians discuss the intricacies of this question, women are left to decide whether to

abort a fetus which results from rape with little moral guidance
or pastoral help from the church.

32. Otto A. Piper, *The Biblical View of Sex and Marriage* (New
York: Charles Scribner's Sons, 1960), p. 62.

33. *Ibid*.

34. *Baker's Dictionary*, p. 319; *Dictionary of Moral Theology*,
p. 614.

35. *Dictionary of Moral Theology*, p. 614.

36. Noonan, p. 203.

37. *Ibid*., p. 205.

38. Nelson, p. 105.

39. In this regard, Nelson's discussion in *Embodiment* of "Love and
Sexual Ethics" is most helpful.

40. In some traditions past and present, an additional concern was
the procreative potential of sexual activity, i.e., sexual activity
which could lead to conception within marriage was acceptable while nonprocreative sexual acts were wrong.

41. *Encyclopedia of Bioethics*, p. 1578.

42. *Ibid*., p. 1582.

43. Arlene Swidler, "It's No Sin to Be Raped," *U.S. Catholic* (February 1979), p. 12.

44. In fact it is seldom the case that women who are raped are
engaged in "morally suspect" activity. For these victims, it is
especially hard to "explain" the rape to others and to themselves.

45. Augustine, *City of God* (London: Oxford University Press,
1963), p. 16.

46. *Ibid*.

47. *Ibid*., p. 17.

48. "Relationship" here is not limited to an intimate primary relationship but refers to any interaction with other persons. "The
experience of relation is fundamental and constitutive of human being; that it is good and powerful; and that it is only
within this experience—as it is happening here and now—that
we may realize *that the power in relation is God*." Carter
Heyward, *The Redemption of God* (Washington, D.C.: University Press of America, 1982), pp. 1–2.

49. This theological insight is concretized in the covenant. "Cove-

nant" is used in Scripture to describe the relationships among people and between people and God.

50. "A variety of polar concepts can thus be used, bearing common meanings with different shadings: sin and salvation, alienation and reconciliation, fragmentation and wholeness, death and life, law and gospel, death and resurrection." James Nelson, p. 72.

51. Nelson, p. 72.

52. "Bodily integrity" is a term used by social ethicist Beverly Wildung Harrison to describe the right (particularly for women) to control one's own body and to establish personal physical boundaries. "Theology of Pro-Choice: A Feminist Perspective," *The Witness*, vol. 64 (September 1981), p. 20.

53. Carter Heyward, *The Redemption of God* (Washington, D.C.: University Press of America, 1982), p. 18.

54. A. Nicholas Groth with H. Jean Birnbaum, *Men Who Rape* (New York: Plenum Press, 1979), p. 4.

55. It should be no surprise that when there is no intervention or assistance, some victims (mostly male) grow up to become offenders. The sins of the fathers are truly manifest in the sons.

56. Genesis 34: 7; 2 Samuel 13: 12; Deuteronomy 22: 21; Judges 19: 23–24, 20: 6.

57. "Folly" defined as "wickedness or wantonness."

58. I have not attempted here to address the ways in which the legal system itself contributes to justice or injustice in resolving incidents of sexual violence. A guilty plea or a conviction may be the first step toward acknowledging the wrong done, moving the offender to repentance, and changing treatment or incarceration.

59. "The ten years' experience of rape crisis centers have shown that the large majority, 90%, of the rapes committed are intra-racial, confined within racial groupings, as opposed to the dominant myths that most rapes are inter-racial." Loretta J. Ross, "Rape and Third World Women," *Aegis*, no. 35 (Summer 1982), p. 46.

60. "African women in America are eighteen times more likely to be rape victims than our white counterparts." Bella Hooks,

Ain't I a Woman: Black Women and Feminism (Boston: South End Press, 1981), quoted in Loretta J. Ross, "Rape and Third World Women," *Aegis*, no. 35 (Summer 1982), p. 41.

61. This is changing as more and more people of color are staffing and volunteering in these agencies.

62. Alice Walker, "Advancing Luna—and Ida B. Wells," *You Can't Keep a Good Woman Down* (New York: Harcourt Brace Jovanovich, 1982), p. 93.

63. "The racist nature of the criminal justice system still has a drastic impact on Third World communities as non-white men are disproportionately jailed for sexual assault. . . . According to the Federal Bureau of Prison reports, in Florida between 1940–1946, of the 125 white males who raped white women, 6 (about 5%) received death penalties. Of the 68 African males who raped African women, 3 (about 4%) received death penalties. Of the 84 African males convicted of raping white women, 45 (about 54%) received death sentences; not one of the 8 white offenders convicted of raping African women received a death sentence. These figures vary little throughout the country, and as a matter of fact, no white male has ever been sentenced to death for the rape of a non-white woman in the history of America." Loretta J. Ross, "Rape and Third World Women," *Aegis*, no. 35 (Summer 1982), p. 45.

64. For example, Susan Brownmiller in *Against Our Will*. See critique in Lynora Williams, "Violence Against Women," *The Black Scholar* (January–February, 1981), p. 21.

65. This requires inclusion of women of color as staff and volunteers in rape crisis centers.

66. For additional information on sexual violence and black women, see Angela Davis, "The Dialectics of Rape," *Ms.* Magazine (June 1975), pp. 74 ff.; Gerta Lerner, ed., "The Rape of Black Women as a Weapon of Terror," *Black Women in White America: A Documentary History* (New York: Vintage Books, 1972); Beverly Smith, "Black Women's Health: Notes for a Course," *But Some of Us Are Brave* (Old Westbury, N.Y.: The Feminist Press, 1982), pp. 112–13.

Chapter 4

Consensual Sex and a New Sexual Ethic

Because of the persistent confusion between sexual activity and sexual violence, any discussion of the ethical questions posed by sexual violence must also include a discussion of contemporary sexual ethics. The confusion of sexual activity with sexual violence has prevented many people from realizing how frequently their sexual experiences are really experiences of coercive "sex." What is consensual sex? What principles and parameters would support consensual sex between persons?

The Principle of Consent

The principle of consent, fully informed and freely given, in sexual activity should be the basis for any discussion of sexual ethics. Functionally this principle means that a person has the right to say "no" to any form of sexual contact and they have a right to have that "no" respected. Utilizing the principle of consent can assist people in preventing "coercive 'sex'" because it counters the game-playing which encourages the "no really means yes" game.

The corollary to the right to say "no" is the right to say "yes" to sexual activity which is freely chosen.[1] The principle of consent is not anti-sexual. It does not obligate one always to say "no" to sexual activity. It is the right to say "no" and the right to say "yes" when fully informed and freely acting. Sexual ethics has to do with teaching people to make responsible choices based on specific principles and with respecting the other person's choice to say "yes" or "no." The only *rule* that should guide one's sexual decision-making and behavior is "thou shalt not sexually manipulate, abuse, or take advantage of another at any time." Persons have the right, the responsibility, and the capability to make decisions about sexual activity and the right to have those decisions respected; but they can only do this if they have information, self-confidence, and power in their lives. This does not mean that persons will not make mistakes; however, it does assume that people can learn from their mistakes.

Accepting the principle of consent is of special concern with regard to teenagers. Many adults, concerned about preventing teenage pregnancy, sexually transmitted disease, promiscuity, etc., do not feel that teenagers should have the right to make decisions about sexual activity. The solution, according to some adults, is teaching girls to say "no" to *any* sexual contact with boys. Most adults do not suggest teaching boys anything about their responsibilities in these matters. The suggested solution reinforces a damaging double standard in which females are expected to be responsible for male sexuality. Once again males are not to be held accountable for their sexuality. Furthermore, this "solution" is unrealistic. Teenagers will have some form of sexual contact with peers or adults. Our concern should be whether they experience that contact as consensual and responsible, or coercive and abusive. The nature of this experience will shape their learning about themselves as sexual beings. Unfortunately, they run a high risk of being confronted with a sexually abusive situation.

Working with teenagers on the topics of sexuality and sexual abuse is difficult because their sexual development is in a formative state. They are at different points in their individual development; they are experiencing increased physical and emotional responses, they are bombarded with messages which attempt to shape their consciousness and self-image, and many do not have a strong sense of self-respect and confidence. Unfortunately, for many (especially girls), their first "sexual" experience is an abusive one: child molestation, obscene phone calls, flasher encounters, acquaintance rape, incestuous abuse. These experiences invariably present themselves as "normative," i.e., "this must be what sex is all about, something over which I have no control and no choice." Experiences of sexual abuse can have a lasting impact which make an adjustment to a responsible and fulfilling sexual life later on difficult. This is why it is necessary to have an alternative, positive image of sexuality. Providing teenagers with information and the sense that sex is a gift from God intended to be shared responsibly in relationship to another is one of the most effective means of *preventing* sexual abuse and sexual violence. Perceiving sex in this way teaches teenagers that they have a right to bodily integrity and a need to respect the bodily integrity of others.

If the principle of consent is accepted as the standard for sexual activity and if it is recognized that in order for consent to be meaningful, it must be considered in relationships of equal power, then we must realize that the vast majority of social and sexual relationships between women and men in our society have the potential to be nonconsensual, i.e., coercive and abusive. Moreover we can see why it has been so easy to confuse sexual activity with sexual violence: Freely chosen, fully informed, and mutually agreed upon sexual activity with another might in fact be a rare experience. Coercive and abusive sexual activity may be the norm and thus the most common experience for both women and men. The model of consensual sex is seldom promoted or encouraged in this society.

Applying the Principle of Consent in Relationships of Unequal Power

Ethical discussions dealing with the principle of consent involve us in the subtle complexities of sexual activity. For example, a 12-year-old girl who is approached sexually by her uncle does not have the information she needs to choose to consent. Moreover she does not have the power in that relationship to refuse consent and have her choice respected. Due to her age and naiveté and to her subordinate status in relation to her uncle she is being coerced.[2] Similarly, a client in counseling with a therapist or pastor does not have the strength and freedom to withhold consent to sexual advances. Most people in counseling are feeling vulnerable to begin with and the therapist or pastor represents a role of authority and power which can easily be misused to coerce a sexual encounter. Neither an employee approached sexually by a supervisor nor a student approached by a teacher has the needed prerequisites for giving freely chosen consent to sexual contact. By nature of their position vis-á-vis the person who approaches them, they do not have the option of choosing to consent or withhold consent. The wife whose husband demands sexual access to her at any time under threat of a beating may have sufficient information, but she does not have the freedom to withhold consent. She believes her only option is to submit.

The key element in these interactions is power and powerlessness. Anytime a person is in a position subordinate to another, that person is vulnerable to exploitation and abuse and the person in the dominant role has the potential to misuse the power by coercing the subordinate—child, teenager, or adult. The failure to understand the principle of consent in the context of unequal power in sexual relationships contributes to several forms of sexual abuse which are difficult for some to see as abusive. Because of this there are some who are engaged in misguided advocacy for the acceptance of incest, marital rape, and sexual contact between clients and pastors or therapists.

The movement advocating the benefits of incestuous sexual activity between adults and children is one such area. The movement has come to be known as the "Pro-Incest Lobby."[3] Proponents of this position argue that sex between adults and children causes no harm and is beneficial because touching, affection, and intimacy strengthens family love and discourages teenage promiscuity and rebellion. While some of those now seeking to legitimize incest are genuinely concerned about the lack of physical affection in families, their solution misses the point. There is a significant difference between affectionate physical contact and sexual contact. In the latter, the needs of the adult family member are met to the detriment of the child. Children know the difference. They know when an adult is giving them affirmation through affection and when they are being used sexually by the adult. They know the difference between an affectionate kiss on the cheek and a French kiss, or the difference between a hug and a hand creeping up the inside of their thigh.

Discussion of affection in the family often raises the defenses of parents who are concerned that their children develop healthy, open attitudes about sexuality. Such parents may give their children lots of physical affection, openly discuss sexual topics, and often are casual about nudity in the home. More than other parents these parents are likely to recognize their own sexual feelings toward their children. These feelings are neither unnatural nor uncommon. However, acting on these feelings to the benefit of the parent and the detriment of the child is abusive. The parent has the responsibility *not* to act sexually toward the child in order to protect the child.

It appears that those who are "pro-incest" have never had clinical experience working with victims or offenders of incestuous sexual abuse. They also seem to ignore the abundance of current research and writing in this area. The "Pro-Incest

Lobby" is speaking out of a vacuum—flailing at a non-existent taboo which they see as an outdated religious and moral hangup standing in the way of sexual freedom and fulfillment. They extrapolate data from cross-cultural studies of sexual behavior and apply an inappropriate remedy for our society's difficulty in expressing affection through physical contact.

For those with clinical experience dealing with victims and offenders, the issue is not affection or conformity to expectations of church or society. The issue is one of abuse and exploitation. Incest, or any form of adult-child sexual contact, takes advantage of a child who is both uninformed and powerless. The child is uninformed simply by nature of being young and lacking the information held by adults. In addition, because the adult has authority over the child, the child is powerless to give or withhold consent to sexual activity. Without consent, the sexual encounter is abusive for the child. Sexual contact between persons is appropriate only when both persons are fully informed and freely choose such contact. This choice is only possible when both persons have the power to choose and to have the choice respected. Children do not have this power in relation to adults, especially with adults who are parents or parental figures. Even when a child solicits sexual contact with an adult or parent, it is the adult's responsibility to protect the child from an experience which is certain to create lasting psychological problems. Although a child *may* initially see an incestuous experience as positive because she/he is receiving a great deal of attention from an adult, almost all eventually see it as negative. They feel confused, exploited, or even fearful. The negative psychological effects are difficult to overcome and may last a lifetime (See Chapter 8, "Responding to Child Sexual Abuse.")

The pro-incest supporters believe that adults have the right to do whatever they wish with children's bodies. The active, vocal promotion of incest in the media by supposed authorities supports the message of magazines like *Hustler* which portray sexual contact between adults and children in cartoons, and the actions of those sexually abusing their children.

Instead of a "pro-incest lobby," we need two things: First, a *sexual ethic which clearly and unequivocally requires consent*. Sexual contact between persons is appropriate only when both persons are fully informed and freely choose such contact. This choice is only possible when both persons have the power to choose and to have the choice respected. Children do not have this power in relation to adults. Second, a *taboo against abuse* is necessary. Children are fragile and vulnerable in many ways and deserve the protection of adults until they are old enough to have the power to act on their own behalf. Adults have the responsibility not to take advantage of this special status by sexually using a child. A strong and consistent message is needed that children are to be protected from abuse and that being an adult, especially a parent, carries with it the responsibility to protect children— abuse is taboo.

Marital rape represents yet another contemporary problem that runs counter to the principle of consent in sexual relationships. The predominant attitude is reflected in state laws that say that rape cannot occur between husband and wife since a husband always has the right to sexual access to his wife. In fact rape within marriage occurs in at least fourteen percent of marriages.[4] If we define rape as the forced penetration by the penis or any object of the vagina, mouth or anus against the will of the victim, then it does not matter what the relationship is between the victim and offender. Marriage does not make forced sexual intercourse "sex" rather than rape. Marital rape is a prime example of the confusion between sexual activity and sexual violence.

Cultural attitudes, often supported and encouraged by religious teachings, have sustained the long-standing belief that there is no such thing as marital rape. The church is partially responsible for conveying the notion that husbands have conjugal rights and wives have conjugal duties. This belief can lead to coercive sexual activity on the part of the husband. Yet on this point, Scripture is explicitly mutual:

> The husband should give to his wife her conjugal rights, and likewise the wife to her husband. For the wife does not rule over her own body, but the husband does; likewise the husband does not rule over his own body, but the wife does. Do not refuse one another except perhaps by agreement for a season, that you may devote yourselves to prayer; but then come together again, lest Satan tempt you through lack of self-control. I say this by way of concession, not of command.
>
> I Corinthians 7:3–6

Both parties, according to Scripture, have the right to engage in sexual activity or to refuse to engage in sexual activity. The principle of consent should apply to any sexual relationship and certainly to marriage.

Sexual contact between pastors and parishioners or pastoral counselors and clients is a growing problem which is slowly being acknowledged by the religious community.[5] This problem occurs most often within a counseling relationship and represents a violation of the principle of consent. When people seek help from a pastor, they are emotionally vulnerable and confused. The clergyperson is in a position of authority and is seen as having more knowledge than the one seeking help. In this counseling relationship, the pastor has greater power, and so, a professional responsibility to be of assistance and not to take advantage of that power. When a pastor or pastoral counselor engages in sexual activity with a parishioner or client, the pastor/counselor takes advantage of his/her role in authority, betrays the trust placed in him/her by the parishioner or client, and exploits the vulnerability of that person.[6] This experience can leave the parishioner or client feeling betrayed, exploited, guilty, and confused. Rather than receiving help, the person is further confused and traumatized.

This situation is not exclusively a problem for professional clergy. Other professional groups experience similar situations. Doctors, therapists, and similar professionals also are finding the problem of sexual contact with patients and clients to be a serious issue of professional ethics. The dynamics are similar. What is unique for clergy (and potentially more damaging for the parishioner or client) is the additional authority role which clergy carry as "God's representative" within the religious institutions and groups which they serve. Also, unlike any other professionals, parish pastors have access to people's lives: They can initiate visits and contact with parishioners whether or not it is requested. All of this means that being approached sexually by or having sexual contact with one's pastor is even more confusing and disruptive than in a secular setting. The additional burden for the parishioner or client is a sense of being betrayed not only by the minister but also by God and the Church. Finally, and perhaps most tragically, this betrayal by one's pastor represents a major obstacle to the parishioner or client's personal faith. The damage to one's spiritual life done by this experience is often profound and long term.

The issue is one of professional ethics. A pastor or pastoral counselor is called to be pastor or counselor and is, in this role, entrusted with the emotional and physical well-being of those he or she serves. Professional ethics require that this role be maintained and that this trust be upheld.

Initiating or participating in sexual activity with one's parishioner or client is a violation of professional ethics on two levels. First, it is a violation of role. One cannot be a pastor / counselor for a person and at the same time be a lover / sexual partner with that person. These two roles cannot be fulfilled responsibly simultaneously because they represent two different types of relationships. A counseling relationship is by definition a relationship of unequal power in which the needs of the client / parishioner are the priority. A love / sexual relationship is ideally a mutual and equal relationship intended to meet the needs of both persons involved. Second, sexual activity with a parishioner or client is a violation of trust. In a professional relationship, the parishioner or client should be able to trust that a pastor or pastoral counselor will not take advantage of their vulnerability. To do so is to violate the trust relationship between them.[7]

The stereotype often put forth when this issue is discussed says that, on occasion, a minister's judgment slips and he finds himself unwisely involved in a sexual relationship with a parishioner or client. The stereotype contends that this is a one-time event from which the minister recovers when he realizes his mistake. After all, everyone makes mistakes. However, this picture does not fit reality. In fact, it appears that most of the professionals who do engage in sexual activity with clients are repeat offenders. They are persons who seem to be attracted to the helplessness and vulnerability of their parishioners or clients. They do not hesitate to misuse the power and authority of their professional role to coerce or manipulate that person into a sexual relationship. Furthermore, they minimize and deny responsibility for such misconduct. The result is an abusive relationship in which the parishioner or client feels victimized and betrayed.

Sexual contact between client and professional is clearly regarded as unethical and unprofessional in the secular professions (such as medicine, psychiatry, psychology, and social work) and is addressed as an ethical concern by the profession of pastoral counselors. For parish pastors, however, there is less clarity and there are few, if any, guidelines. For parishioners in particular there is little awareness that any sexual approach by a pastor is a violation of professional ethics. Moreover, there is no sense of what recourse a person has when faced with such a situation.

The problem of sexual contact between counselors/pastors and clients/parishioners is becoming increasingly apparent. Yet it represents an area of coercive sex or sexual abuse which remains difficult for many, including its victims, to recognize and address directly. The powerlessness which a person feels in the face of her therapist or pastor, especially when that person represents an institution like the church, is overwhelming. This problem is a profound violation of professional ethics and the principle of consent.

Principles, Rules, and Conditions

Traditionally, sexual ethics have attended to the wrong questions and consequently, the wrong boundaries for sexual behavior have been established. Sexual ethics need to deal more directly with issues of consent and power, and with the potential for exploitation and abuse. Given this context, appropriate rules can be developed to assist individuals in decision-making and to help establish cultural norms which can support these individual decisions. Cultural norms are needed which clearly indicate that "coercive sex" or sexual abuse in any form is unacceptable behavior for anyone.

The principle of consent in sexual activity provides the context for an important rule for sexual behavior: "Thou shalt not sexually manipulate, take advantage of, or abuse another person at any time." While rules are not generally an effective way of practicing ethics, in the case of sexual violence, rules can represent a helpful way of establishing boundaries for personal sexual decision-making. Rules do not solve the complexity of the choices facing an individual, but they can help a person sort through the factors involved in order to make a responsible decision whether or not to engage in sexual activity. One might then argue that, all things being considered equally, this rule is a sufficient guideline: all one need do is check one's motives, find out if the other is consenting, and proceed to negotiate sexual activity. All things are not often equal, so this rule alone is insufficient for many situations. Likewise it is not always easy to establish absence of consent. Some additional boundaries need to be applied.

The primary area in which we need to establish clear boundaries is in situations where there is *by definition* a difference in power between the two persons in the relationship. The factors which can determine a difference in power are age, size, gender, and role. The following relationships may include all of these factors: a 35-year-old father and his 4-year-old daughter; a 55-year-old male therapist and a 28-year-old female client; or a 40-year-old male professor and a 25-year-old female graduate student whom he supervises. Generally speaking, sexual contact between persons where there is this kind of power discrepancy cannot *with any certainty* be consensual. This is because consent requires full knowledge *and* the power to say "no." In such relationships where there is virtually no way to guarantee that the one in a more powerful position will not take advantage of the other person, regardless of conscious intent, it is more just (as well as more pragmatic) to avoid any sexual contact. In the case of adult-child, the mandate not to engage in sexual activity is especially strong because the adult has the responsibility to protect the child who is uninformed, immature, and powerless vis-á-vis adults. Under no circumstances is adult-child sexual contact acceptable—it is unacceptable because it is nonconsensual and exploitative of the child, not because it is sexual. In adult-adult relationships, the responsibility may be less clear but no less important. Even though expressed consent and desire for sexual contact may be mutual, the primary difference in power has to be considered.

As individuals, we have a responsibility to set boundaries on our sexual activity in order to avoid imposing nonconsensual, coercive sexual activity on another person. With an equal, we have the responsibility to negotiate sexual activity and to respect any expression of nonconsent he/she may make. With an adult or child over whom we have authority or power, we have the responsibility to avoid initiating sexual contact or responding to the initiation of sexual contact from them. This does not mean that people do not have sexual feelings for their children or students, clients or parishioners, and employees or supervisees. These feelings are natural and not unusual. It does mean that under no circumstance should these sexual feelings be acted on. Since within the Christian tradition we believe that we are created and blessed with the power to choose, we are likewise given the power and responsibility to choose wisely. Also, we are mandated to protect the less powerful from injury or exploitation. Thus, when we choose, we can and must set boundaries on our individual and collective sexual activity in order to apply the principle of consent. This makes possible the creation of a context of right relation in which to engage in sexual activity with another. Agreement in the community regarding these boundaries will create new norms which will encourage individuals to set limits on their behaviors. A new sexual ethic based on the principle of consent can be a significant contribution to eliminating the suffering caused by coercive sexual activity.

Notes

1. Accepting the option to say "yes" carries with it responsibilities, such as protecting oneself against disease and unwanted pregnancy.
2. David Finkelhor's fine article provides an excellent argument for the consent standard to be applied to sexual contact, especially between adults and children. See "What's Wrong with Sex Between Adults and Children? Ethics and Problem of Sexual Abuse," *American Journal of Orthopsychiatry*, no. 49 (October 1979), pp. 692–97.
3. Much of the material on the "Pro-Incest Lobby" appeared in "Working Together," the newsletter of the Center for the Prevention of Sexual and Domestic Violence, vol. 2 (December 1981–January 1982).
4. This figure is based on a 1977 study of 930 women in San Francisco. See Diana E. H. Russell, *Rape in Marriage* (New York: Macmillan, 1982).

5. Material on sexual abuse by clergy and counselors appeared in "Working Together," the newsletter of the Center for the Prevention of Sexual and Domestic Violence, vol. 3 (November–December 1982).
6. In the majority of cases of this kind, the pastor is male and the parishioner or client is female.
7. This is very similar to the expectation that a child should be able to have that her/his parents will not take advantage of her/him by initiating sexual activity.

Chapter 5

RAPE IS AN UNNATURAL ACT

Some of the current research and writing about sexuality and sexual violence provide valuable resources in understanding sexual violence and distinguishing it from sexuality.[1] The field of scientific study has not always been a helpful resource in this regard; often it has done much to create and sustain the confusion of sexual activity with sexual violence. The earliest psychological discussions of sexuality amount to an elaborate apologia for male sexual aggression. In Kathleen Barry's discussion of the ideology of cultural sadism[2] there even appears to be a grand conspiracy on the part of Sigmund Freud, Havelock Ellis, and others to justify male sexual aggression. They defended the sexual violence of the Marquis de Sade and viewed him as a liberator who fearlessly overcame sexual repression. Their work on sexuality contributed heavily to the "normalization of sexual violence," i.e., male sexual aggression being regarded as normal, healthy, and natural.

Early psychological theories viewed the male sex drive as uncontrollable;[3] consequently, according to those theories, men could not be held accountable for what they did. De Sade's erotic life was the ultimate manifestation of this belief. He was convinced that no limit should be placed on his efforts to satisfy his sexual drives and to achieve his own sexual pleasure—even though his pleasure came from acts of violence toward others. He had no trouble justifying assault against women:

> It appears beyond contradiction that Nature has given us the right to carry out our wishes upon all women indif-

113

> ferently; it appears equally that we have the right to force her to submit to our wishes, not in exclusivity, for then I would contradict myself. . . . It is beyond question that we have the right to establish laws which will force women to yield to the ardors of him who desires her; violence itself being one of the results of this right, we can legally employ it. Has not Nature proved to us that we have this right, by alloting us the strength necessary to force them to our desires?[4]

By defining sexual aggression and sadism as "natural" and a male prerogative, the apologists sucessfully removed men's responsibility for their sexual behavior. Freud concurs: "The sexuality of most men shows an admixture of *aggression*, of a propensity to subdue, the biological significance of which lies in the necessity for overcoming the resistance of the sexual object by actions other than mere courting."[5] And Barry concludes:

> Freud's theories of sexuality and sadism are totally deterministic: people act from an undefinable instinct and an unknowable unconscious which was determined in unremembered sexual drives of infancy. The responsibility for behavior is moved from the individual to the instinct and the unconscious. Both sadistic and masochistic behavior are defined in terms of unconscious instinctual *needs*. The concept of unconscious instinct precludes morality and divorces psychology from the concept of victim or assailant. The social situation or milieu, the conditions that give rise to sexual violence have been reduced to a discussion of internal psychological mechanisms.[6]

If we then add the erroneous belief that women are by nature masochistic and unconsciously desire to be raped and beaten, we have a perfect match. Men are naturally sexually aggressive and desire to subdue and dominate women and women love that kind of treatment. If this is the case, then there is really no such thing as sexual abuse and violence; there is no offense, there are no victims, and no offenders. There is no need for an ethical discussion.

Fortunately Kinsey challenged this notion with the thesis that sexual interest and erotic response are learned.[7] Yet this insight does not solve the problem created by Freud and others because their *belief* in natural, uncontrollable male sexual aggression is part of what is learned. Barry comments:

> The first definitive experiences of the fully developed, learned sex drive are in adolescence when, according to Kinsey, the time between sexual stimulation and response is shortest. From cultural myths boys readily learn, first, that this drive is one that must be fulfilled because it cannot be contained and, second, that they have the implicit right to take girls and women as objects to fulfill that drive. Sexual power is thereby conditioned in the sex experience of adolescent boys. While boys are experiencing and experimenting with their sexuality, the culture provides them with substantive images of idealized sexual encounter; they often learn that they must live up to pornographic models of sex. As boys, growing into men, experiment with their sexuality free from both restraint and responsibility, that mode of behavior becomes, unchanged, the basis of adult male sexual power.[8]

She suggests that oftentimes men are simply suffering from arrested sexual development:

> Learned, impulsive, uncontrollable adolescent male sex drive has become for many men the mode of their adult sexual behavior. It is *arrested sexual development,* which stems from a sexuality that has not grown beyond what was acted out at age 12, 13 or 14. Arrested sexual development defines the context for all aspects of their behavior . . . It explains the self-centered, exploitative, and bullying behavior that characterizes pimps, procur-

ers, rapists and wife beaters. These men have learned to take immediate sexual gratification and ultimately any other form of gratification in whatever way they choose.[9]

There is a basis in male sexual socialization for attitudes which perpetuate the confusion between sexual activity and sexual violence. However, these beliefs about male sexuality can no longer be regarded as truths about male sexual nature.[10]

The belief that male sexual aggression is natural, biologically driven behavior and "is so overwhelming that the male is the one to be acted upon by it"[11] is a myth that we can no longer afford to perpetuate. It feeds a whole other set of myths about sexual violence: for example, that rape is primarily a sexual act brought on by sexually provocative women and that rapists really are men who cannot help themselves.

Fortunately those who have worked with sex offenders in the last ten years provide us with a more accurate and insightful understanding of the pathology of offenders. In the writings of clinician Nicholas Groth, we find a clear understanding of rape as a pseudosexual act motivated by aggression and hostility.[12] Likewise, in the accounts of victims and offenders we find valuable evidence of a distinction between sexual activity and sexual violence. Following is the testimony of an offender:

> I was enraged when I started out. I lost control and struck out with violence. After the assault, I felt relieved. I felt I had gotten even. There was no sexual satisfaction; in fact, I felt a little disgusted. I felt relieved of the tension and anger for a while, but then it would start to build up again, little things but I couldn't shake them off.[13]

> The crime itself just frustrated me more. I wasn't sexually aroused. I had to force myself. I felt some relief coming off because there was some tension release, but very shortly afterwards the feelings were worse. I blamed the victim and felt it was her fault and that a

different girl would give me the satisfaction I craved, so I
went out looking for another victim.[14]

For victims, the most common reaction to rape is "I thought I
was going to be killed." Fear rather than pleasure predomi-
nates regardless of the actual circumstances of the rape itself.
Central to this fear is the loss of power in determining one's
life and the loss of bodily integrity. Terror and powerlessness
shape the victim's experience of rape. Children who suffer
sexual abuse express fear and/or confusion and always a sense
of exploitation and loss of control. Contrary to the myth, there
is no masochistic delight experienced by victims of sexual
assault.

Persistence in believing that sexual violence is primarily
sexual in nature leads to the erroneous conclusions that it is
then inevitable; that rape is part of human nature; that all men
are rapists; that biology is destiny. New anthropological evidence makes clear that there are cultures where rape is virtually nonexistent. Peggy Reeves Sanday's cross-cultural studies
of rape[15] suggest that rape is hardly universal. Sanday found
that in forty-seven percent of the societies she studied, rape
was absent or rare. Seventeen percent were "rape-prone" and
used rape to punish women. Thirty-six percent were
categorized as "rape-present," i.e., rape exists but the incidence is unclear. Sanday concludes that rape comes not from
a biological drive but is a learned response which comes from
the way societies are organized. Certain behavioral patterns
and attitudes are common to rape-prone societies.

> [These societies] tolerate violence and encourage men
> and boys to be tough, aggressive, and competitive. Men
> in such cultures generally have special, politically impor-
> tant gathering spots off limits to women, whether they
> be in the Mundurucu men's club or the corner tavern.
> Women take little or no part in public decision making
> or religious rituals; men mock or scorn women's work
> and remain aloof from childbearing and rearing. These

groups usually trace their beginnings to a male supreme being.[16]

In contrast, rape-free societies (such as the Ashanti of West Africa) evidence respect for women as influential members of society, a primary female diety or a male/female diety, full participation of women in religious life with an equal role in ritual activities, cooperation between women and men in work and decision-making, and harmonious existence with the environment. Women's qualities of nurture and fertility are highly valued. In this context of socialization for men and women, rape becomes an aberration.

Although rape is not a given in male human nature, it is a given in our culture, so much so that it is difficult to imagine what life would be like without sexual violence. The fact that sexual violence is endemic to our society leads people to conclude that it must be natural. There are those whose self-interest is served by persisting in this belief. If rape is natural and therefore inevitable, then men who rape never have to take responsibility for their behavior. All society can ever hope to do is to control or limit sexually violent behavior; it can never hope to eliminate it because, well, men are just like that. In other words, men are a hopeless, lost cause and sexual violence is a fact of life.

It is curious that those who seem to have the most hope for men, those who are in effect willing to say that not all men are rapists, are feminists who believe that rape is not inevitable but rather is unnatural. Basic to this belief is the conviction that men can and must take responsibility for their behavior, especially their sexual and aggressive behavior. Feminists are the most critical of contemporary social mores and have greater expectations of men as a group than does the rest of society; inherent in this position is a high regard for men. It assumes that men, like women, are capable of responsible human interaction and it expects responsible behavior from men as well as women.

For women, the question of whether or not sexual violence

is natural male behavior is an issue of basic survival. If women accept the belief that sexual violence is natural, i.e., part of the created order, then women must also accept that it is God's will that they exist in an alien and hostile environment and are always at risk of attack by men. While many women's experience may be that they do exist in such an environment, accepting this as a natural and God-given reality is fatalistic and self-defeating because it discourages women from changing their environment.

The theological implications are profound: If sexual violence is part of the natural, created order, then women are created to be victims and are *by their nature* always at risk on a cosmic as well as a mundane level. This assumption requires an understanding of God as one who is hostile and cruel to have created two classes of persons—the victims and the victimizers. Nothing in the core of Jewish or Christian beliefs can substantiate this conception of God's nature or human nature. Our Scripture does not begin with "In the beginning God created victim and victimizer and saw that it was good," but rather, "In the beginning God created humankind, male and female."

If we understand the metaphor of the Fall as a way of conceptualizing the realization of free choice for humankind, we can begin to understand the nature of sin. Free choice includes the option of choosing to victimize another. When a person is so alienated from God and his neighbor that he chooses to strike out, seeking violent conquest rather than loving union with another, he is manifesting the brokenness of humankind and establishing a relationship of victim and victimizer. If we regard this relationship as anything other than a manifestation of brokenness and therefore unnatural and not God's creation, then we allow it to be normative, to shape our relationships, and to deny the New Covenant promised by Jesus. Regarding rape as an unnatural act means that neither women nor men must accept the roles of victim and victimizer as God-given and unchangeable. The cycle need not continue.

Notes

1. For example, A. Nicholas Groth with Jean Birnbaum, *Men Who Rape* (New York: Plenum Press, 1979), and Bernie Zilbergeld, *Male Sexuality* (Boston: Little, Brown, and Company, 1978), pp. 12–20.
2. Kathleen Barry, *Female Sexual Slavery* (Englewood Cliffs, N.J.: Prentice Hall, 1979), pp. 174–214.
3. For example, Theodore Reik, *Psychology of Sex Relations* (New York: Rinehart, 1945), p. 9; and Havelock Ellis, "Analysis of Sexual Impulse," in *Studies in the Psychology of Sex*, I, Part Two (New York: Random House, 1942), p. 65 as quoted in Barry, p. 217.
4. Marquis de Sade, from "La Philosophie Dans le Boudoir," in *Marquis de Sade: Selections*, ed. Paul Dinnage, pp. 132–33, as quoted in Barry, p. 190.
5. Sigmund Freud, *Three Contributions to the Theory of Sex* (New York: E.P. Dutton, 1962), p. 22, as quoted in Barry, p. 193.
6. Barry, p. 193.
7. *Ibid.*, p. 218. Masters and Johnson's work is based on this thesis as is Zilbergeld's sex therapy. Zilbergeld comments: "Human sexuality is basically a learned phenomenon. Very little of our sexual behavior can properly be called instinctive." *Male Sexuality*, p. 12.
8. *Ibid.*, pp. 218–19.
9. *Ibid.*, p. 219.
10. But these myths are still held as truths by many. For example, a psychologist made the following statement in response to a discussion on sexual harassment in the work place: "Every psychologist knows that biologically driven behavior [i.e., sexual] will occur in spite of proscriptions and restrictions."
11. Barry, p. 217.
12. Groth with Birnbaum, p. 2.
13. Quoted in Groth with Birnbaum, p. 15.
14. *Ibid.*, p. 27.
15. As reported in "Rape Free or Rape Prone," by Beryl Lieff Benderly in *Science* (October 1982), pp. 40–43.
16. Benderly, p. 42.

Part 2

A Pastoral Perspective

I NEED STRENGTH. I NEED COMFORT. BUT WHERE CAN I
TURN? MY FAITH PROVIDED STRENGTH AND COMFORT
IN THE PAST. IT WAS MY SANCTUARY. BUT NOW I FIND
MY CHURCH EXPOSED AS A TRAITOR. IT FACILITATED,
JUSTIFIED AND THEN IGNORED MY ABUSE . . . I MUST BE
ANGRY . . . MY ANGER GIVES ME STRENGTH TO STOP
BEING A VICTIM. PLEASE LISTEN TO WHAT I AM ANGRY
ABOUT . . . DON'T FEED ME THE SAME OLD EASY AN-
SWERS. THEY NEVER DID REALLY WORK AND NOW I
KNOW THEY'RE LIES. BUT I DON'T WANT TO GIVE UP MY
SPIRIT. I NEED IT . . . HELP ME TO BE STRONG. HELP ME
TO HAVE COURAGE . . . I AM IN A DARK TUNNEL TRAVEL-
ING VERY FAST AND I CAN SEE NO END. HELP ME BE-
LIEVE I WILL SURVIVE. DON'T MINIMIZE MY PAIN BY
SPEAKING QUICK PLATITUDES. DON'T TRY TO MAKE ME
STOP HURTING SO YOU DON'T HAVE TO SEE IT. AC-
KNOWLEDGE MY PAIN. HURT WITH ME. I NEED TO
KNOW I'M NOT ALONE. BE WITH ME.

"A Plea to My Pastor," from
I Choose to Remember, the Violet
Collective, Minneapolis, 1981.

"AND WHO IS MY NEIGHBOR?" JESUS REPLIED, "A MAN
WAS GOING DOWN FROM JERUSALEM TO JERICHO, AND
HE FELL AMONG ROBBERS, WHO STRIPPED HIM AND
BEAT HIM, AND DEPARTED, LEAVING HIM HALF DEAD.
NOW BY CHANCE A PRIEST WAS GOING DOWN THAT

121

ROAD; AND WHEN HE SAW HIM HE PASSED BY ON THE
OTHER SIDE. SO LIKEWISE A LEVITE, WHEN HE CAME
TO THE PLACE AND SAW HIM, PASSED BY ON THE OTHER
SIDE. BUT A SAMARITAN, AS HE JOURNEYED, CAME TO
WHERE HE WAS; AND WHEN HE SAW HIM, HE HAD COM-
PASSION, AND WENT TO HIM AND BOUND UP HIS
WOUNDS, POURING ON OIL AND WINE; THEN HE SET HIM
ON HIS OWN BEAST AND BROUGHT HIM TO AN INN, AND
TOOK CARE OF HIM. AND THE NEXT DAY HE TOOK OUT
TWO DENARII AND GAVE THEM TO THE INNKEEPER, SAY-
ING, 'TAKE CARE OF HIM; AND WHATEVER MORE YOU
SPEND, I WILL REPAY YOU WHEN I COME BACK.' WHICH
OF THESE THREE, DO YOU THINK, PROVED NEIGHBOR
TO THE MAN WHO FELL AMONG THE ROBBERS?" HE
SAID, "THE ONE WHO SHOWED MERCY ON HIM." AND
JESUS SAID TO HIM, "GO AND DO LIKEWISE."

Luke 10: 29–37

Jesus teaches Christians to respond to the needs and hurts of
their neighbors. When the neighbor is a rape victim or a child
victim of sexual abuse, it is not easy to know how to respond.
These situations often seem unfamiliar, disturbing, or too
complicated for a pastor or layperson. Yet there is a need for
each individual in the community of faith to adopt the role of
the Good Samaritan and not pass by on the other side. The
task is not easy. The needs of victims and their families are
often great and may seem overwhelming: crisis intervention,
support, advocacy, information, spiritual guidance, justice-
making, etc. The needed response to offenders and their
families is equally complex: to make justice, to support repentance and restitution, and hopefully to enable movement
toward healing and reconciliation. The key to a capable and
effective response is for both pastor and congregation to work
together to be well-informed and prepared to help.

It is not unusual for victims of sexual violence to feel abandoned or betrayed by the church. In the past the clergy and lay have been unprepared to help and so have too frequently not been able to respond helpfully. Platitudes are an easy recourse that tell victims they will not receive any real understanding or support from the source. Platitudes work well to keep victims' experiences aloof from the speaker so that he/she can slip by and remain uninvolved. Visualize the Priest on the road to Jericho passing along platitudinous advice as he makes his way around the injured person: ". . . Keep praying. God will take care of everything . . . Read your scripture every day . . . Everything will be fine . . . God hears your prayers . . ." The church can and should be the Samaritan, willing to stop and to expend energy and resources to help victims of sexual violence. Both clergy and laypersons have this pastoral responsibility. In Chapter 6 ("Role of the Minister"), the particular dimensions of the minister's responsibilities when faced with a situation of sexual violence are put forth. In the chapters which follow, the role of the minister (ordained and lay) is discussed in more detail as it relates specifically to victims (Chapter 7, "Responding to Rape Victims" and Chapter 8, "Responding to Child Sexual Abuse") and offenders (Chapter 9, "Responding to Sex Offenders") and to particular religious and spiritual issues (Chapter 10, "Religious Concerns and Pastoral Issues"). Finally, the collective role of the church as pastoral support (Chapter 11, "Community of Faith") and agent for change (Chapter 12, "Strategies for Action") is developed.

Chapter 6

ROLE OF THE MINISTER

Why would someone who has been raped or someone who has sexually abused another go to a minister for help? For some people, the Church is a primary reference point in their lives. When faced with a personal crisis they turn first to their minister. For them, the minister is a trusted and known resource; they assume that he/she will know what to do in this situation. For others, the minister may be the only resource. In a small town or rural area which does not have specialized community services (e.g., a Rape Crisis Line), the minister is the only "helper" available. Still others may seek out a minister because this crisis of sexual victimization is also a crisis of faith. The experience may have raised basic spiritual questions for which the victim or offender needs counsel.

Often ministers are avoided by individuals or families coping with the trauma of sexual violence. Many clergy say that they have never had someone involved in rape or sexual abuse come to them for assistance. Furthermore, they conclude that there is no one in their congregation who is a victim or offender. Given the large numbers of persons who have experienced sexual violence, this assumption is questionable. The more logical conclusion is that many people hesitate to go to their minister when faced with such an experience.

There are several reasons for this hesitation. Generally, any experience of sexual abuse or violence is stigmatizing for the victim. Although society's attitudes are slowly changing, many victims are still afraid to tell anyone about their abuse, because they fear disbelief, judgment, ostracism, and lack of support. Unfortunately, the Church has adopted an attitude, not unlike society's, which says that experiences of sexual abuse or violence are unmentionable and unacceptable in the Church. (See Chapter 11, "Community of Faith.") When the minister and congregation do not initiate discussion of sexual violence, the silence reinforces the stigmatization. Thus, for many the Church and the minister (as representative of the Church) are not viewed as potential resources in this situation.

Another reason for hesitation on the part of the victim or offender may be a perception that the minister lacks knowledge, sensitivity, and/or experience in dealing with sexual assault. A level of trust between pastor and parishioner which is adequate to other situations may not be adequate to this one. The victim or offender fears that the minister will not understand or know what to do. Or perhaps the minister will be so surprised and shocked, that the person seeking help ends up having to help the minister deal with his/her reaction.

Finally, female victims are often hesitant to go to their minister because their minister is male. Having a male minister may heighten the victim's fear that he will not understand or respond sensitively. A clergywoman is often preferred because the victim feels her chances of being understood are better.

The concerns that victims or offenders express about a minister's possible insensitivity are real and reasonable. When one is facing a personal crisis of this magnitude, it is not a good time to risk rejection or lack of understanding from one's minister. So for many people the silence continues. They do not seek help at all. A minister can open the door and let it be known that he/she is available to help with the problem of sexual violence by giving permission for the subject to be discussed in Church and by being prepared to help.

Giving Permission

At the end of a four week seminar on sexual and domestic violence, a Lutheran pastor of a small congregation reported with some distress that in the past several weeks he had had a rape and two incest cases in his congregation. He could not understand why this "sudden outbreak" of sexual abuse in his congregation had occurred. The seminar coordinator explored this further with the group and discovered that the pastor, on the first Sunday after the first seminar session had announced from the pulpit that he was taking a seminar on sexual abuse and domestic violence which he was finding very helpful. In the weeks following that announcement, parishioners came forward for the first time with their concerns about sexual assault. Rather than "a sudden outbreak," each shared a past or chronic unresolved problem.

By making that announcement from the pulpit, the pastor in effect hung up a sign saying, "I am learning about these problems, I know that some of you are facing them, and I am available to help." It should have come as no surprise that people sought his assistance.

Giving permission to victims or offenders to seek help regarding sexual violence happens when the minister communicates that it is acceptable to talk about sexual violence in church and that he/she has the knowledge and expertise to help. This can be accomplished through a sermon, adult/youth/child educational presentations, fliers posted in the narthex advertising local resources like a Rape Crisis Line, use of denominational curricula dealing with the topic, etc.

Being Prepared to Help

It is unlikely that any minister is adequately prepared to respond to a victim or offender of sexual violence unless he/she has had some means to increase his/her knowledge and counseling skills in this area (special training, experience, materials, etc.) The topic remains unmentionable in most seminaries or ministry training programs. While most seminaries and training programs offer education in counseling and crisis intervention, this is not sufficient preparation to respond to sexual violence. Although sexual assault and abuse have some similarities with other life crises, they are, in many ways, unlike any other experience that a person will face. Some degree of specialized knowledge is necessary in order to respond effectively.

A minister must be comfortable with the issue of sexual violence in order to help the victim or offender. Talking with a victim or offender is often a very disquieting experience. The minister may be reminded of her/his own experience of violence or abuse as a victim or an offender. The important thing is that the minister be aware of those feelings and of their source in his/her experience. For example, if a minister has been a victim of sexual assault or abuse, she/he may be better prepared to empathize with a victim. Or, if the personal pain of the experience is still acute, it may have the opposite effect of blocking the minister's response. In this case, it is advisable that the minister refer the victim to another minister who is more able to respond.

The minister may be confronted with things which he/she does not want to hear, experiences which are horrendous and disturbing. The temptation is to minimize or not believe what is being said. Some of the stories may seem "unbelievable," i.e., things we would like to believe are not happening to people, but in fact are. For example, the daughter of the sunday school superintendent who ran away from home finally returns only to reveal to the minister that she ran away because her father was sexually abusing her. Such a situation has numerous ramifications and no simple solutions. While the gut reaction might be disbelief, horror, and minimization, none of these is helpful to a victim.

Developing a level of comfort can be accomplished by exploring one's experiences with, feelings about, and attitudes concerning sexual violence. Ministers (and other helpers) need to reflect on several questions: To what extent does the minister identify with the victim or with the offender? What personal experiences of the minister relate in some way, for example, when has the minister felt powerless, frightened, or alone? What beliefs about sexual violence does the minister have which are not based on fact, for example, the belief that some women ask to be raped or rapists are just sexually over-active? A minister can respond calmly and yet not minimize the situation by being knowledgeable about the subject of sexual violence, knowing what to do next, and not allowing feelings of anger, disgust, disbelief, or discomfort to dominate the response.

Reassurance and Support

Following a sexual assault, victims need to hear that they are acceptable and worthy persons, that they are not to blame for their assault, and that they will not be abandoned in this crisis. The minister's efforts to reassure and support a victim in these ways are much more meaningful if the congregation is also able to be supportive. Then the minister can communicate that the church as a whole is prepared to be with the victim through this experience. (See Chapter 11, "Community of Faith.")

One frequent question is whether a male minister can be of assistance to a female victim of sexual violence. The concern raised by this question is whether or not the maleness of the minister may be too great an obstacle to the victim's feeling comfortable and trusting with him. Following the assault, some victims find it very difficult to feel safe talking with any male helper be it police, medical personnel, or clergy. In such instances, the sensitive male minister can refer the victim to a qualified female minister or laywoman. For other victims, it can be reassuring to talk with a male they trust. In these cases, it is important that the minister avoid reacting in a patronizing or protective manner. A victim needs someone who can listen and be supportive rather than someone who wants to rescue her from the experience. When giving support, the male minister should avoid any action which might be perceived by the victim as physically or sexually threatening; thus, touching should be kept to a minimum.

A male clergy colleague told of his initial meeting with a 23-year-old woman rape victim. As they talked in his office, he got up from his chair, walked around behind her and put his hands on her shoulders to reassure her and offer her physical support. She froze and stopped talking with him. His action was frightening and threatening to her. The man who had raped her had approached her from behind. His action toward her, although well-intended, was entirely inappropriate and counterproductive. Reassurance and support may best be communicated in nonphysical ways.

Initial Assessment

During the initial meeting with a victim or offender, the minister needs to assess several areas in order to determine his/her appropriate role in the particular situation. If the assault occurred within the past 48 hours and if no other resources (rape crisis agency, police, medical personnel) have been contacted, then the minister should assume a crisis intervention role. The way that the minister will carry out this role will depend on what community resources are available for referral and on who the person is—victim or offender. (See Chapters 7, 8, and 9 on victims and offenders.) If the assault or abuse is chronic (incestuous abuse) or has occurred earlier in the person's life, then the minister's response will be less crisis-oriented and more focused on assessing the current needs of the person seeking help and the impact of the sexual violence on that person's life.

If other crisis resources have been contacted and are being utilized, then the minister's attention will be directed towards areas not covered by those resources, particularly spiritual or religious concerns. (See Chapter 10, "Religious Concerns and Pastoral Issues.") In either case, the minister's role in assessing the situation is a critical one. This is especially true if the minister is the only person who has been told about the assault or abuse.

Working with Other Community Resources

Most urban and suburban communities now have sexual assault services available, either through a crisis line, a community mental health center, or a specialized service such as a rape crisis center. Services for sex offenders are not as common, but are sometimes available regionally. Persons providing these services are trained to respond to sexual violence whether it is a crisis or chronic problem. They are available as resources to ministers and congregations.

A COOPERATIVE STYLE

Unfortunately, some ministers hesitate to utilize secular resources in response to a problem like sexual assault. A gulf seems to have developed over the years between mental health/social services and religious professionals, resulting from long-standing mistrust and skepticism. Social workers and counselors do not trust ministers to know what to do when faced with sexual assault or abuse, and ministers do not trust social workers and counselors to be sensitive to the spiritual needs of their parishioners. This attitude of mutual mistrust comes from experiences of poor communication, insensitivity, inappropriate treatment or counsel, etc., on both sides. The resulting lack of cooperation means that persons who need help are placed in a position of choosing either social services and counseling or pastoral support. In some communities, little effort has been made by either side to overcome this gulf and to begin to relate to each other as professional peers who have special training and skills much needed by the people they serve.

In other communities, both clergy and secular resources have sought to bridge the gap and there has been remarkable success in sharing resources and in developing a network of services. They work cooperatively in response to victims and offenders. For example, in one particular community, a group of ministers has been trained by the rape crisis center to deal with sexual assault. In turn the rape crisis center staff/volunteers have been trained by the ministers to respond sensitively to the religious concerns expressed by victims. Here, a mutual referral agreement exists where ministers refer victims for crisis counseling to the rape crisis center and the rape crisis center refers victims with religious questions to the ministers. In addition, ministers help with fund raising and community education and encourage lay participation in the center as volunteers.

Seldom does a minister have the training, time, and energy to adequately provide the immediate and long-term counseling which a victim or offender may need. A network develops when religious and secular professionals reach out to each other as peers, sharing information, providing training for each other, serving on boards of agencies, and offering to provide services when referred to by the other. Working together to meet the needs of victims and offenders begins to build the mutual trust that is needed for effective work.

KNOW YOUR RESOURCES

Research conducted in 1977 in a large urban area indicated that seventy-six percent of parish ministers in that area did not know of a single resource (general or specialized) which they could call upon to assist victims or offenders of sexual violence. At that time, this city had the highest concentration of sexual assault services of any area in the region. Yet parish ministers were not utilizing these services because they did not even know what was available.[1]

It is often up to the minister to find out what services are available in his/her community. A minister should contact any agency which sounds like it addresses sexual assault and request copies of brochures to keep on hand. If possible, go and talk to an agency staff person in order to clarify what they do offer. Attend any training events offered by the agency. Know and use the resources in the community.

Making Referrals

When resources are available, it is preferable to refer a victim or offender to a specialized agency prepared to deal with sexual assault. The staff and volunteers of these agencies have the knowledge and experience to provide the needed counseling and advocacy. They know the medical and legal systems and can minimize the difficulties that a victim may face dealing with them.

In making a referral to an agency, it is preferable to refer to a specific person who is known and trusted by the minister. This is another reason to get to know an agency's staff and volunteers either through self-introduction or through participation in a conference or training workshop. Giving a victim or offender a name of someone at the agency reassures them that they will connect with an individual who can help.

A minister's wise use of referrals comes from an awareness of his/her limitations and from a clear understanding of what his/her role should be. Particularly from a parish minister's point of view, limited expertise, time and energy necessitate utilization of all available resources.

PASTORAL ROLE

The minister, in a pastoral role, can offer a victim or offender a unique resource. His/her expertise in pastoral care, theology, and ethics can be invaluable to a religiously-affiliated person facing the aftermath of a sexual assault. The minister is the primary resource when a victim or offender faces questions such as: Why did God let this happen to me? Does God still love me? Can God forgive me for this? Through prayer, spiritual counsel and reflection, and Scripture study, the minister can assist a person with primary issues in her/his life. (See Chapter 10, "Religious Concerns and Pastoral Issues.")

When a minister makes a referral to a secular agency, this does not mean that the minister's responsibility ends. The pastoral and supportive role is often still needed by the person seeking help. A minister who tries to pass total responsibility on to another helper is said to be "dumping the client." Even if the religious concerns seem to be initially resolved, it is important to check in with a victim for the next six months to a year, reminding her/him of the continuing care and support of the church. For an offender, weekly contact may be necessary to insure that he remains in treatment and to assure him of the support of the church as he goes through that rehabilitation process.

CONFIDENTIALITY

While all helping professionals have a responsibility to maintain confidentiality regarding interaction between them and their clients, clergy have an additional responsibility within the context of a pastoral and confessional role. There are a number of states which recognize the special nature of the clergy-penitent relationship and provide the legal privilege for clergy not to be forced to divulge information learned within a pastoral relationship.[2] In sexual assault situations this can sometimes create a bind for the minister. On the one hand, there is the minister's commitment not to repeat information shared in a counseling or confessional setting. On the other hand, when information comes from an offender or relates to the sexual abuse of a child the minister has an ethical responsibility to do whatever is necessary to prevent any further assault or abuse from occurring. This may involve reporting information to a law enforcement agency.

In some states, clergy are required by law (along with teachers, social workers, doctors, counselors, etc.) to report any suspicion of child abuse (including child sexual abuse) to a law enforcement or child protection agency. In other states, clergy are exempt from this reporting requirement. Suspicion or confirmation that sexual abuse has occurred, coupled with the knowledge that unless the offender is stopped, he will offend again, press a minister to choose between conflicting ethical principles. Shall the pastor break confidentiality in order to protect a child or shall he/she safeguard confidentiality and place the child at further risk? In this case, concern for the welfare of potential or actual victims takes precedent. This is particularly true for child victims who are at high risk and often powerless to stop the abuse. Acting on this concern may then mean reporting an offender to the authorities. This action is also a function of concern for the welfare of the offender. His confession or indication that he is sexually offending may be a call for help. This help is only possible if he is held accountable for his acts and provided with appropriate treatment. (See Chapter 9, "Responding to Sex Offenders.") For his sake as well as the sake of the victim, it is the pastor's responsibility to intervene to stop the offender's abusive behavior. Allowing him to continue to offend with our knowledge is unfair to him and only multiplies the legal difficulties he will face.

The church has addressed the question of confidentiality. Within the Anglican Communion the "Seal of Confession" is defined as follows:

> The absolute obligation not to reveal anything said by a
> penitent using the Sacrament of Penance. . . . The obli-
> gation arises from a tacit contract between penitent and
> confessor, from its necessity for maintenance of the use
> of the sacrament by the faithful, and from canon law. The
> obligation covers direct and indirect revelation, e.g., un-
> guarded statements from which matters heard in con-
> fession could be deduced or recognized, and admits of
> no exception, no matter what urgent reasons of life or
> death, Church or state, may be advanced.[3]

The Roman Catholic provision is equally stringent. The
United Methodist Book of Discipline is more straightforward
but also strict: "Ministers of the United Methodist Church are
charged to maintain all confidences inviolate, including confessional confidences."[4] Some denominations have addressed
the issue with limited conditions.

> In keeping with the historic discipline and practice of the
> Lutheran Church and to be true to a sacred trust inher-
> ent in the nature of the pastoral office, no minister of
> The Lutheran Church in America shall divulge any
> confidential disclosure given to him in the course of his
> care of souls or otherwise in his professional capacity,
> except with the express permission of the person who
> has confided in him or *in order to prevent a crime*
> [emphasis added].[5]

This provision is very important in questioning the absolute
nature of pastor-penitent privilege when communication is
exchanged which indicates that there will be further sexual
assault or abuse. It is important for the Church to face the
conflict in ethical values which results from an awareness of
sexual assault or abuse committed by a counselee or penitent.

When a minister feels an ethical mandate to report knowledge of sexual abuse or assault, it need not be done in such a
way as to deceive the offender; it need not be done se-
cretively. Rather the minister should inform the person at the

time the information is shared that it needs to be reported to
the appropriate authorities. The pastor can then ask the person's permission to notify police or a child protection service.
Or the pastor can suggest to the person that it is in their own
best interest to report it himself/herself (in the presence of
the minister). These approaches hold the greatest potential
for maintaining some level of trust between minister and offender. In this way an ongoing relationship between minister
and offender may be maintained and effective intervention
can be carried out to stop the abuse.

Working Alone: A Rural or Small Town Setting

Ministers serving in a rural area or small town may find that
they are *the* primary resource for victims or offenders. In this
case, they may be called upon to provide crisis counseling and
support as well as advocacy with medical and legal systems.
This can be a very demanding role. The minister needs to
keep in mind his/her time and energy limitations and develop
additional support resources within the congregation. (See
Chapter 11, "The Community of Faith.") Ideally, members of
the congregation can assist, for example, by accompanying a
victim to a medical appointment or prosecutor interview. The
pastoral role of providing spiritual guidance and counsel is
basically the same as for the urban/suburban minister. For
the rural minister, this role may be more integrated into the
overall assistance he/she provides for the victim, offender,
and their families.

Often confidentiality arises as an additional complication in
a rural or small town setting. Where everyone knows everyone else and news travels fast through informal networks of
communication, it is difficult to keep anything confidential.
Fears about having their experience become public knowledge may prevent victims from seeking help from clergy,
police, or doctors in their own community. Ministers espe-

cially need to be sensitive to this fear so that a victim can be assured that confidences with her/him will be respected. A minister should specifically mention his/her awareness of the need for extra care in safeguarding the privacy of a victim and assure her/him that he/she will not share any information about the victim's situation without her/his permission. The minister should be careful not to share *any aspect* of a story which might identify the victim.

An additional responsibility which may arise for the rural minister in response to an incident of sexual violence is the need to minister to the community as a whole (if news of the incident becomes public). The community may react with some of the same characteristics as the victim: fear, panic, anger, grief, etc. The local minister(s) can provide factual information about sexual violence, help direct the community's anger in appropriate channels to minimize tendencies toward revenge, and generally assist the community in working through its feelings.

Notes

1. This research was conducted by Denise Hormann for the Center for the Prevention of Sexual and Domestic Violence. Partial results were published in JSAC *Grapevine*, vol. 11, no. 3 (September 1979), pp. 1–2.

2. There is a great deal of controversy surrounding this provision, including the question of who is a clergyperson, what about clergy in churches which do not have a doctrine of sacramental confession, what about nonsacramental confidential communications, etc. For additional discussion of the legal issues involved, see Seward Reese, "Confidential Communications to the Clergy," *Ohio State Law Journal*, vol. 24 (1963), pp. 55–88.

3. *The Oxford Dictionary of the Christian Church* 1234 (London: 1957) as cited in Seward Reese, "Confidential Communications to Clergy," *Ohio State Law Journal*, vol. 24 (1963), p. 68.

4. *The Book of Discipline of the United Methodist Church* (Nashville, Tn.: United Methodist Publishing House, 1980), para. 440.4, p. 220.

5. The Minutes of the United Lutheran Church in America, the 22nd Biennial Convention, 1960, at 277, as quoted in Reese, p. 69.

Chapter 7

RESPONDING TO RAPE VICTIMS

A 62-YEAR-OLD WOMAN WAS BROUGHT TO THE HOSPITAL AT 8:30 A.M. BY THE POLICE. SHE HAD MULTIPLE BRUISES ON HER FACE, NECK, CHEST, AND BACK, AS WELL AS A 2-INCH STAB WOUND IN HER ABDOMEN. HER FIRST WORDS TO THE COUNSELOR WERE, "I THOUGHT I WAS GOING TO BE KILLED. I DIDN'T WANT TO DIE—I DIDN'T THINK IT WAS MY TIME, BUT I REMEMBER THINKING THIS IS THE WAY I WAS GOING TO DIE. . . ."

Ann Wolbert Burgess and Lynda Lytle Holstrom,
Rape: Victims of Crisis

MY GOD, MY GOD, WHY HAST THOU FORSAKEN ME
AND ART SO FAR FROM SAVING ME, FROM HEEDING
MY GROANS? . . .

MY STRENGTH DRAINS AWAY LIKE WATER
AND ALL MY BONES ARE LOOSE.
MY HEART HAS TURNED TO WAX AND MELTS WITHIN
ME.
MY MOUTH IS DRY AS A POTSHERD,
AND MY TONGUE STICKS TO MY JAW;
I AM LAID LOW IN THE DUST OF DEATH.
THE HUNTSMEN ARE ALL ABOUT ME;
A BAND OF RUFFIANS RINGS ME ROUND . . .

Psalm 22:1, 14–16 (NEB)

THE WOMAN ARRIVED AT THE EMERGENCY WARD AT 3:30 A.M. ACCOMPANIED BY HER BOYFRIEND. SHE SAID THE MAN WHO ASSAULTED HER HAD BEEN A PREVIOUS BOYFRIEND OF HERS FOR A 1½ YEAR PERIOD AND THAT

HE HAD COME TO HER APARTMENT UNINVITED THAT
EVENING. SHE SAID, ". . . HE GAVE ME A SHAKEDOWN.
HE KNEW WHERE TO HIT ME AND HOW TO GET ME
SCARED SO I WOULD DO WHAT HE TOLD ME, AND I DID
. . . I'M NOT SUPPOSED TO TELL. HE SAID HE'D BEAT ME
IF I TELL . . . YOU KNOW, THEY WORK YOU OVER—TO
CONTROL YOU—SO THEY CAN HAVE YOU SEXUALLY ANY
TIME THEY WANT. HE HIT ME ON THE EAR, PULLED MY
HAIR, HIT ME IN THE BACK BY MY KIDNEYS—VERY
STRATEGIC. BUT IT'S NOT THE PHYSICAL PART THAT'S
THE THING—IT'S THE MENTAL CONTROL OVER YOU . . .
I WONDER HOW MANY WOMEN ARE BEATEN LIKE THIS
AND NEVER TELL. BUT I'M NOT SAFE, I HAVE TO TELL
. . ."

Ann Wolbert Burgess and Lynda Lytle Holmstrom,
Rape: Victims of Crisis

To fulfill the pastoral role with rape victims, one must understand fully the nature of rape, its impact on the victim, and
the healing process.

Nature of Rape

The nature of the rape situation itself is significant in shaping
a helpful counseling response. Rape experiences generally fall
into two broad categories: blitz rape and confidence rape.[1]
Blitz rape is the sudden, surprise attack by a stranger or
strangers. Totally unexpected, the rape shatters the victim's
sense of trust in her/his environment. The victim may feel
that she/he was in the wrong place at the wrong time. She/he
is unable to make sense out of what has happened to her/him.
The blitz rape may occur outside (park, alley, etc.) or inside
(home, school, church, office, etc.) In either case, the victim

is taken by surprise. In the blitz rape, the victim feels betrayed by her/his environment which she/he once trusted. The world is no longer safe and hospitable. Counseling issues should focus on grieving the loss of safety and security, acceptance of the reality of a hostile environment without being unnecessarily limited by it, and learning to take risks again.

The *confidence rape* involves a rapist and victim who have had some degree of contact prior to the assault. The degree of previous contact varies.

- New acquaintance—A rapist may approach a victim in a seemingly safe situation, begin a conversation to develop trust on the part of the victim, and then betray that trust by taking advantage of the victim. For example, a new acquaintance rapist might be someone seeking information from a person waiting for a bus; a delivery or repair person; a friend of a friend who just moved to town.
- Friend or family member—This rapist may be a neighbor, date, friend, classmate, co-worker, family member, etc. The rapist has some kind of prior relationship with the victim, which he uses as a way of establishing trust and then betrays. The rapist does not respect the bounds of the relationship or the wishes of the victim. The victim of this rapist in particular may be hesitant to seek assistance or report the assault because she/he feels that no one will believe it was rape since she/he had a relationship with the person.
- Authority figure—In this case the rapist is a person who has authority over the victim and abuses that authority by sexually assaulting the victim, sometimes referred to as "getting sexual favors." This rapist could be an employer, doctor, minister, counselor, teacher, etc.

In addition to the blitz and confidence rape situations described above in which it is assumed that the victim was capable of expressing an unwillingness to have sexual contact, some rapes occur when a victim is unable to express lack of consent to sexual contact. This could occur in a blitz or confidence situation. Sexual contact without expressed unwillingness often involves children who, due to their lack of maturity and awareness, are unable to freely choose or resist sexual contact. (See Chapter 3, "Responding to Child Sexual Abuse.") For example, a 4-year-old girl who simply does not know enough to comprehend what a 16-year-old babysitter is doing to her much less express lack of consent; or a 10-year-old boy whose father not only demands sexual contact with him but threatens to beat him if he does not comply. Likewise, adults may be unable to express lack of consent or to effectively resist unwanted sexual contact if they are developmentally disabled, intoxicated, or drugged. For example, a 30-year-old woman confined to a wheelchair by cerebral palsy; or a 40-year-old man who passes out drunk at a party. In all of these situations, a rapist can easily take advantage of a person who is in a vulnerable position. The counseling response for victims who were unable to express lack of consent should focus on clarification that what occurred was a violent assault, that the victim was not to blame for it but rather was taken advantage of while in a vulnerable state.

From Victim to Survivor

Although rape which culminates in the death of the victim is relatively rare, the life-threatening dimension of the experience of rape is very real and quite common. Fear, both during and following the assault, is the most widely reported reaction. In addition, the victim's entire world is turned upside down. She/he has experienced the something that she/he thinks only happens to other people, the something that contradicts the ordinary "rules" of one's environment. The world is no longer a hospitable place. A rape victim's life will never be the same again.

In discussing the impact of rape, it is difficult to accurately convey the magnitude of the experience without falling prey to perpetuating the stereotype of the female victim whose life has been destroyed or who has been driven to the edge of insanity by the rape. Permanent, crippling damage to the victim is rare. Rape is not the worst thing that can happen to a person. However, rape is horrendous and destructive for any victim. Like other crimes of violence, rape leaves the victim with that sense that "I could have been killed." The physical, emotional, and spiritual violation is overwhelming. But whether or not that damage becomes permanent depends largely on the response of those around the victim and the process of recovery which she/he experiences.

The process of recovery from the rape begins immediately. The thing that is most important in shaping that recovery is the response which a rape victim receives from family, friends, the Church, and the community. If she/he feels comfortable in sharing what happened with those around her/him and finds a sensitive and caring response, then the recovery process proceeds. If, for any reason, the victim cannot share the experience and seek support from such resources, then the recovery may be long and painful; the negative impact of the rape is maximized by the victim's isolation.

Support and understanding from family, friends, or helpers enables a rape victim to utilize his/her own strengths to move through recovery and to discover new strengths and learnings which result in growth and change. There are many examples of this growth and change. One victim discovered that with the support of an advocate, she could deal with the legal system which had always intimidated her before. Another victim found that his family was able to support him in a way he had never expected and, consequently, a new level of family relationships resulted. One woman discovered that her anger was a positive, energizing emotion which she need not fear any longer. A victim who managed to fight off her assailant realized that she could effectively protect herself. Another victim decided that she need not tolerate an abusive relationship with her boyfriend. It is through such recovery processes that victims become survivors, no longer victimized by the rape experience. *Without* supportive responses from family, friends, church, and community, all too often victims remain victims.

Victims may have unrealistic expectations of the people around them. They may want a rape crisis worker to take care of everything (police interview, medical appointments, etc.), or a clergyperson to make it all better, or a friend to "solve" all their problems by rescuing them. These expectations are understandable but are not in the best interest of the victim. Those who are trying to help need to be realistic about what they can provide: time to listen, genuine caring, information, advocacy, support. They also need to be careful not to be pulled into rescuing the victim. Rescuing perpetuates the victimization by treating the victim as helpless and ignoring the person's inner strengths. The goal is not to rescue but to assist the victim in moving through the crisis to become a survivor.

Whether a clergyperson or lay counselor is working in conjunction with rape crisis services or is the only available resource to the victim (see preceding chapter) he/she needs to understand the impact of the rape as a particular form of crisis experience. The remainder of this chapter will discuss rape as a crisis using the Rape Trauma Syndrome as a paradigm and suggesting appropriate counseling interventions to be used by a helper/counselor in responding to the rape victim.

Rape as a Crisis

A crisis is defined as an externally imposed event that creates a situation beyond a person's normal coping threshold which requires problem solving abilities beyond that person's capacity at that particular time. It presents a person with a situation in which the person feels powerless, overwhelmed, and out-of-control of her/his life. When faced with a crisis like divorce, terminal illness, natural disaster, etc., most people first seek help from familiar resources like friends or family (primary resources). Next, they may go to individuals or agencies which are seen as trustworthy but not particularly familiar to the person in crisis, like clergy or police (secondary resources). As a last resort, they may call upon groups that are anonymous and unfamiliar like the Red Cross, foodbanks, Crisis Line, etc. (tertiary resources).

Unlike victims of other crises, many rape victims hesitate to approach primary resources for help for fear of being rejected or not believed or being blamed for the attack. Thus, they are more likely to utilize secondary or tertiary helpers first. Regardless of whom they approach—clergy, police, medical personnel, family, or friends—*it is strongly recommended that that person encourage the victim to contact a local rape crisis service to assist with the initial crisis intervention*. The specialized counseling and advocacy services available through such agencies are invaluable for the victim.

RAPE TRAUMA SYNDROME[2]

The research conducted by Burgess and Holmstrom in 1972–1973 provided the first comprehensive theoretical model through which to understand the experience of rape from the perspective of the victim. They interviewed rape victims who sought assistance from Boston City Hospital during this period and, based on their analysis of this data, developed the concept of the Rape Trauma Syndrome. This paradigm remains a most helpful means to understanding the impact of rape on a victim. Understanding what a "typical" victim's reaction to rape is enables a more realistic response on the part of helpers, family, and friends. It provides helpers with a way of anticipating some of the needs of a victim as she/he moves through the recovery process. The discussion which follows draws heavily on Burgess and Holmstrom's material.

The Rape Trauma Syndrome occurs in two phases. The acute phase is the initial period in which there is much disruption in the victim's life during which fear remains the primary emotion. The reorganization phase begins two to three weeks after the rape, during which the victim begins the recovery process of reorganizing her/his life.

The **acute phase** may last from a few days to a few weeks. The initial reaction to the attack is usually expressed in one of two ways. Some victims freely express their feelings such as fear, anger, anxiety, confusion, and despair by crying, laughing, talking, behaving restlessly, etc. Other victims control the expression of their feelings and thus appear calm, quiet, withdrawn, and in control. This type of victim, because she is not behaving "like a victim," i.e., crying hysterically, is sometimes not seen as credible. ("If she has been raped, why isn't she upset?") Both the expressive and controlled reactions are quite common.

During the acute phase, victims will often experience *physical reactions*.

- Trauma or injuries sustained during the attack remain painful.
- Sleep pattern disturbance: The victim may sleep all the time or not be able to sleep at all.
- Eating pattern disturbance: The victim may overeat or have no appetite.
- Symptoms specific to the attack: Vaginal or anal irritation are common; forced anal sex may cause rectal bleeding; forced oral sex may result in a sore throat.

There is a wide range of *emotional reactions* as well.

- Fear of the physical violence and the possibility of death: There may also be the fear that the rapist will return and rape again, based on the rapist's threat that he will come back if the victim tells anyone.

- Humiliation, shame, embarrassment: Because of the way in which society has traditionally responded to rape victims, the victim may feel stigmatized, as well as feeling embarrassed by the sexual nature of the attack.
- Guilt and self-blame: Again, society tends to blame the victim, which leads victims to blame themselves, i.e., "if only I hadn't done such and such . . ."
- Anger: Angry feelings may be stifled during the acute phase, but will almost always surface at some later point. The anger is legitimate and healthy, and often energizes the victim to an active response: "I am really mad. My life is disrupted; every part of it upset. And I have to be grateful I wasn't killed."
- Mood swings: These may be extreme and sudden, which may be very stressful for a counselor or family member trying to help.
- Inappropriate expressions of feelings: Feelings expressed may seem out of proportion to a particular situation, e.g., flying off the handle at an insignificant thing or sobbing in response to a greeting from a friend. These reactions may be stressful for both the victim and those around her.
- Extra caution and distrust: The victim may exhibit what seems to others to be unncessary caution or hesitation, for example, when she is seated, she may not like having someone standing behind her, she may refuse to answer the door, or she may be suddenly overprotective of her children.
- Fear of negative reactions by peers or parents: This is most common for adolescent victims who fear being stigmatized by their peers and being blamed by their parents.

In addition, during the acute phase, a victim may engage in specific *patterns of thought* which any helper needs to be aware of.

- Blocking thoughts of assault: This is one way of coping in which a victim temporarily "forgets" whole parts of the experience.
- Trying to undo what happened: This is an attempt to go back before the assault and recover the safety and security she once knew. It also involves self-blaming: "If only I hadn't opened the door"; "if only I hadn't dated him"; "if only I hadn't hitchhiked." The reality is that the victim may have made some poor choices or unwise decisions; however, this in no way means that she is responsible for the rape. The victim can learn from those choices and decisions and not make the same mistake again.
- Wishing she had handled the assault situation differently: This is expressed in the form of "if only I had screamed"; "if only I hadn't struggled, maybe he wouldn't have hurt me so much." This second guessing of intuitive responses to the attack ignores the fact that she probably did what she could in the face of a situation which presented few options.
- Conflict between intellect and emotion: This may be particularly true for a victim who is mature, aware, and sees herself as well-informed about sexual assault. She "knows" what is happening to her and has a cognitive framework for coping with it; yet her emotional reactions are mixed and intense and at this point beyond her control. This can create frustration for her.

A victim may experience any or all of these reactions during the acute phase. Listen carefully to the victim's feelings and thoughts, acknowledge them as legitimate, and reassure her that her reactions are normal, i.e., common for someone who has experienced rape. This is an important educational function which the pastor or counselor can provide. A victim may be anxious that she "is going crazy" because she has never experienced such a range of emotions before. Reassure her and explain that in her situation, her feelings and thoughts make sense *and* that she will move into the next phase of recovery, the reorganization phase.

The **long-term reorganization phase** lasts anywhere from a few weeks to a year or more. The length of time depends in part on how strong a network of support the victim has, what inner resources she is able to muster, and whether or not effective crisis intervention was available for her at the time of the rape. Reactions during this phase vary; there is no standard pattern to the process.

Changes in Routine. Many victims discover they have a limited level of functioning in their family, job, or school setting. They may have difficulty, for example, organizing the family's holiday gathering, working a regular 8-to-5 day, or studying for their final exams. During this time, they may need someone to help mediate in these situations, relieving them of all but minimal responsibilities. While some victims may need to take just a few days off from family, work, or school, it is important to return to somewhat of a "normal" routine as soon as possible; this helps to establish a sense of order and stability in the reorganization process.

It is very common for victims to make major changes in their routines such as moving their place of residence or changing jobs. The change of residence is particularly important for victims who were attacked in their homes. The fact that the rapist knows where they live magnifies their fear that he may return. Moving is a practical security measure. The move may also include getting an unlisted telephone number.

Many victims seek out extended family for support, regardless of the degree of intimacy they may feel with their families at that time. They may make a visit to family in another part of the country and then may or may not share information about the assault. There is a need to reconnect to a part of their lives which is somewhat stable, secure, and known. Again, this facilitates the reorganization process.

For teenagers, truancy may be a response to the assault.

They may see this as the only way of coping with responsibilities at school and with their fears of being stigmatized by their peers. A supportive, understanding response from parents, rather than a punitive one, will speed the reorganization process and the return to normal school participation.

Dreams and Nightmares. Dreams and nightmares are disturbing to victims because they feel they cannot get away from their experience even in sleep. Initially the nightmares may be vivid reenactments of the rape itself or some variation of a violent attack on the victim. As the recovery proceeds, however, the nightmares change. The victim may relive the event up to the point of the rape and then she fights back, gains mastery over the situation, and injures or kills her attacker.

For some victims this is a necessary and healthy reaction which is an indication that they are regaining a sense of power over their own lives. Some, however, are frightened by their response when they realize their anger and their potential for violence. These dreams will probably begin to dissipate once victims express their anger about the rape and the rapist.

Phobias. The phobias which rape victims develop are defensive reactions which usually have to do with the circumstances of the rape. If the victim was alone when attacked, then she may now fear being alone. If the victim was abducted from a crowd in a public place, then she may now fear crowds. The victim's fear may be specific to the actual place where she was assaulted, or it may be global and non-specific. The basis of many victims' phobias is the very real fear of reprisal from the rapist. While fear is a common reaction, reprisals are not a common occurrence.

A victim may generalize about the rapist's characteristics and fear anyone who resembles him. This is especially difficult for victims assaulted by a man of another race. When this phobia is combined with racial prejudice, it may result in fear and hatred for all men of that race; for example, a black victim who now fears all white men after she was raped by one, or a white victim who now fears all Latino men after her attack. It is important at some point to challenge this generalization on the part of victims in order to minimize their potential for increased racial prejudice.

Many victims indicate phobias related to their sexual lives. If the person has been sexually active, then she may fear attempting to reestablish the sexual aspect of her relationship: How will she react? Will she be responsive and orgasmic? How will she feel about her partner? How will her partner feel about her? The reestablishment of her sexual relationship may be a slow process. If the victim was a virgin, her fears related to sexuality are equally difficult. She can easily conclude that her rape experience is what sex really is: an agressive, abusive act over which she has no control. It is not easy to avoid this generalization, especially in an environment which perpetuates the confusion between sexual activity and sexual violence.

Counseling Implications

Any counseling response to a victim needs to take account of the stages through which the crisis reaction progresses. The initial reaction of a rape victim is *shock and disbelief*. Victims. seldom believe that such a thing can happen to them. Then, as the reality sets in, they begin to face the *awareness* of what has happened. Their reactions include fear, anger, crying, withdrawal, etc. Next comes some degree of *acceptance* of the fact that they live in a dangerous society. This may involve letting go of a somewhat naive view which regarded society as basically safe as long as one was careful. Then there is the stage of *restitution and resolution*. Hopefully, the victim seeks some form of restitution, perhaps through the legal system, and finally comes to some sense of resolution, which enables the victim to live with the reality of the experience, learn from it, and be willing to continue to take risks in order to live a meaningful life.

For victims who were functioning normally and adequately prior to the rape, this experience is best dealt with as a crisis reaction and basic crisis intervention strategies are the best response. The counseling is issue-oriented, short-term, and educational. Long-term psychotherapy usually is not needed.

For victims who have a history of physical or psychological problems (depression, psychosis, drug or alcohol abuse, battering or sexual abuse), their response to the Rape Trauma Syndrome may be a *compound reaction*. Once these multiple problems are identified, multiple resources should be utilized, and long-term therapy with a psychotherapist may be necessary.

Ministers or counselors should be alert to what is called the *silent rape reaction*. The majority of victims never report rape, so it is not surprising that people who seek counseling or assistance for other problems may also be rape victims who have never told anyone and who have been carrying the psychological burden of the experience for months or years. This may also be true for persons who have just been raped and are seeking help, but who were also raped or sexually abused earlier in their lives. Indications of previous sexual assault may be evident in an interview, e.g., long silences, blocking, distress, reports of phobic reactions, fear of relationships with men, loss of self-confidence and self-esteem, feelings of self-blame, nightmares, or sexual dysfunction. If there is a suspicion of previous sexual abuse, ask the victim if she has ever had forced sexual contact or ever been assaulted. This will give her permission to share that information if she so chooses. The counselor can then evaluate what additional assistance may be needed from other sources.

ADDITIONAL COUNSELING CONCERNS

The most common response during the reorganization phase that a rape victim experiences is an effort to make sense out of what happened. This is the primary motivation behind

the "if only I hadn't done such and such . . ." thought process.
If she can just figure out what she did that led to the rape, and
then be certain to never do that again, she will never be raped
again. This line of thought not only gives a victim a sense of
providing for her own self-protection, but also (she hopes) can
help her regain a sense of power and control over her life.
Asking the question "Why did this happen to me?" is both a
practical and philosophical concern. For many, that question
is expressed in religious terms: Why did God let this happen
to me; am I being punished for something? Why is there this
kind of suffering in the world? Is this God's will for my life? If
the victim can comprehend her/his experience within the
cosmic order of things, then she/he will not feel so completely overwhelmed by it. These pastoral issues require an
informed and sensitive response from a pastor or counselor.
They are discussed in detail in Chapter 10, "Religious Concerns and Pastoral Issues."

Long, drawn out legal processes may reactivate the victim's
need for support at a later point in the reorganization phase.
Arrest and prosecution of the offender may take place months
after the assault. Not only can the trial force the victim to relive the crisis of the assault itself, it may also present a new
crisis when it is apparent that the legal system is insensitive
and unresponsive to the needs and rights of the victim. It is
usually a lengthy process which may be particularly frustrat-
ing and painful for the victim. She/he will need additional
support at this time from family, friends, pastor, and counselor.

For a pastor especially, an aspect of the long-term recovery
which may arise is a victim's reaction to anniversaries of the
rape. It is important for a pastor to be sensitive to this possibility because he/she may be the only helper who has an
ongoing relationship with the victim (e.g., if the victim is a
member of the congregation). Like the anniversary of a death,
the anniversary of a rape is a significant time of reflection and
experience for the victim. She may want to recall the details

of the assault, or mark the date in some personal or corporate way in celebration of the progress she has made in recovery and renewal. It might be helpful for a pastor to mark the date on his/her calendar and pay a visit to the victim sometime during the week of the anniversary.

PARTICULAR ISSUES FOR MALE VICTIMS

In general, male victims of rape experience all of the same reactions as female victims, though there are a few additional reactions and problems which are specific to the males who are sexually assaulted. Since most men have been socialized to see themselves as invulnerable to sexual attack, they have rarely thought of themselves as potential victims of sexual violence. Most males never see themselves as powerless or at the mercy of someone else. Rape, in the traditional male understanding, is something that happens to females. Yet men are raped by other men in institutions (mental hospitals, prisons, etc.) and in the general social setting.

When faced with someone bigger and stronger, when threatened with a weapon, or when confronted by a gang, a man may find that he is unable to effectively defend himself against sexual assault. A rape experience threatens a man's self-image and his view of his place in the world, both of which are traditionally defined by his masculinity.

This challenge to one's self-image is particularly apparent in the concerns which male victims, unlike female victims, express about sexual orientation. Many male rape victims have high levels of anxiety about their own sexual orientation following the rape. The anxiety is expressed as a fear that somehow the rape will "turn them into a homosexual" or that they must actually be or appear to be homosexual to have elicited the attacker's attention. This anxiety stems not only from the confusion of sexuality with sexual violence, but is further complicated by the deep fear and misunderstanding of homosexuality which exists in our culture. These particular concerns of male rape victims result primarily from their ignorance about the crime of sexual assault and, thus, can be addressed most effectively through education of the victim. Male rape victims, regardless of their predominant sexual preference, will need assistance in understanding that the motivation for rape is violence and has little to do with their individual sexual identity.

The confused sense of sexuality and identity which male rape victims often experience is compounded by the fact that during rapes, ejaculation and erection on the part of the victim may occur:

> People mistakenly think that if a man is in a state of fear or anxiety, he cannot achieve erection or ejaculation. Further, in misidentifying ejaculation with orgasm, the victim himself may not understand his psychological response and may come to doubt his own sexuality. . . . A male also tends to equate manhood with independence and control, and when such control is lost, as it is in rape, and when another male gains sexual access to him, there may be a feeling of loss of manhood in the victim. He feels less of a man. . . . Whereas a female victim may develop an aversion to sexual relations following an assault, a male victim may show increased need for sexual activity with a woman to reestablish and reaffirm his manhood. Because of existing social values, sexual contact with another male, even though coerced, may be stigmatizing for the victim, since now his manhood has been tampered with, and he himself may fear labeling or even actual conversion, especially if he is not secure in regard to his sexual identity.[3]

In addition, he needs to understand that a sexual assault does not "change" a person's sexual orientation. If he has ongoing confusion or ambivalence about his sexual orientation, the assault may heighten that ambivalence. Such ambivalence about sexual orientation should be dealt with as a concern apart from the assault. This would assist the person in identifying and accepting his own sexual feelings, whether they be homosexual, bisexual, or heterosexual. For the victim who was comfortable with his sexual orientation prior to the rape, the anxiety about the impact of the assault on his sexual orientation will be minimal and he will be better able to focus or his reorganization process.

In the face of confusion on the part of the victim about his sexual identity, it is important for a counselor or helper to assist the victim in understanding that his manhood, or more accurately his personhood, is not based solely on his ability to resist sexual attack. His feelings may be coming more from the socialization he has received about what it means "to be a man" than from what are the real bases of his personhood. He can then focus on the aspects of the rape experience which affect men and women similarly.

The victim who is gay may experience self-blame, anger, and guilt in addition to the trauma of the assault. He may be less likely to seek medical care or to report to the police for fear of the response. He will need support and advocacy in order to get the services he requires. In addition, a gay male victim will be faced with the reality that he is more vulnerable than other men in the community to attack by heterosexual males and that he has less recourse to prevent such attacks. This awareness may present difficulties as he attempts to reorganize his life following the assault.

In addition to all the concerns discussed above, men who are raped in the correctional or institutional setting also have to face the fact that they remain at high risk for further assault. The rapist has regular access to them and they have few effective means of protection from the assailant. In this setting, rape takes on the larger function of establishing a pattern of social power and hierarchy among males in a closed system. (See Chapter 9, "Responding to Sex Offenders.") Thus the physical and psychological trauma to the victim may be more severe and long term than for men raped in the community.

Finally, because the social attitude toward homosexuals is

still so negative, and because the social definition of masculinity remains so rigid, the stigmatization of male rape victims is even greater than for females.

When confronted with the reality of male victimization, the public response is usually one of incredulity, skepticism, and derision. The consequence of this is that very few male victims talk about their experiences or seek assistance from friends or community resources. They end up trying to cope with the victimization in complete isolation, with no support and little information that could help them clarify the experience and begin the process of recovery. The more openly male sexual victimization is discussed, the more likely it is that men will come forward to seek assistance.

Family Reactions

Family reactions to the rape are often very strong and have a significant impact on the victim's recovery. Anyone with whom the victim has a significant family relationship (partner, parent, sibling, etc.) and with whom the victim has shared some information about the rape, will experience some degree of family reaction to the news. Sometimes physical and emotional reactions mimic those of the victims, e.g., sleeplessness, headaches, loss of appetite, excessive fears. While these reactions are very real and legitimate, it is important to remind the family member who the victim is. For example, the mother of a 14-year-old rape victim said to the minister, "I can't believe this happened to me." The minister replied, "It didn't happen to you. It happened to your daughter and she needs you to support her now." This is not to deny the impact on the family members. But the crisis belongs to the victim. When other family members take on the crisis as their own, then too often the victim feels a responsibility to stop and take care of them. Thus her/his recovery process is interrupted. A minister can be very helpful at this point in dealing with the feelings of family members apart from the victim so that the family members have someone to talk to in order to be an effective support for the victim.

There are several ways in which family reactions may pose additional problems for the victim. Parents' need to explain the rape may take the form of blaming the victim: "I told you not to go to that party. If you hadn't disobeyed me, this would never have happened." Thus a teenage victim ends up feeling alienated from and punished by her parents at a time when she needs support and understanding. Male family members in particular will often express their anger at what has happened with bravado and talk of revenge. Consider, for example, the husband of a 47-year-old rape victim who says, "I'm gonna find that son-of-a-bitch and when I do I'm gonna fix him so he won't rape again." This reaction on the part of a family member is the most upsetting to a rape victim and presents an additional crisis with which she must cope. She realizes that the angry family member may do something irrational or violent. Such acts would have the potential to create additional problems for her and the family. So her attention is turned to the family member and away from her own needs. An angry, vengeful response by a family member who is unwilling to stop and consider the consequences of his actions is never helpful in resolving the situation or in speeding the recovery of the victim.

The desire for revenge on the part of male family members often arises from a sense on their part that *they* have been violated: "How could that guy do this to *me?*" They perceive themselves as the victim rather than their wife or child. Obviously, such a response is not helpful to the victim. This attitude on the part of the family member should be challenged. He should be reminded that he is not the victim, but that his wife or child is the victim and needs his support. His concern should be for the victim's feelings and how he can be supportive to her. Again, a minister is in a good position to work with the male family member while he expresses and clarifies his feelings and decides what to do about them.

Family members are also affected by and are a part of the reorganization process for the victim, a process that can create additional stress for all the family. For example, a teenage victim may want to change schools in the middle of the year which may involve additional expense and inconvenience for parents. Parents are well advised to be flexible and willing to negotiate changes in the family's lifestyle following the rape, and to seek assistance from a rape crisis agency or minister in dealing with their own feelings about these changes.

Part of the reorganization process for victims involves the reestablishment of relationships with their sexual partners. This can be difficult and stressful emotionally and sexually for both persons. The victim may be emotionally distant; sexual interaction often ceases for a period of time. It takes time for a victim to renew intimacy and trust, to be able to open up emotionally and to be vulnerable with a partner again. Sometimes partners hurry to reestablish their sexual relationship in order to prove to themselves that "everything is alright," that "the rape hasn't changed anything." This is often not the best course. If the sexual encounter is disappointing, both people may have increased anxiety about their relationship. Sometimes male partners of victims experience impotence and discover that they are ambivalent about reestablishing their sexual relationship. In all these circumstances, partners are most successful when they proceed slowly and avoid pushing a false sense of renewed intimacy. It is more productive to focus on the little things that are important to the relationship, e.g., a special place which means a lot to both, a special meal to prepare for each other, etc. Physical affection without sexual expectations can be very reassuring to both partners; it can renew intimacy and prepare both for reestablishing sexual activity. It is especially helpful to discuss feelings and not assume what the other may be thinking or feeling.

Family members may find themselves in a quandary, wanting to help but not knowing how. Guidance from a rape crisis agency or minister can assist them. They may feel anxious because they do not know what to say or how to act: Should they talk about the rape or not mention it? Should they reach out physically to the victim or carefully avoid touching? The victim should choose what she/he needs most from the family. Some victims need to talk about the rape a lot; some need to tell the story only once. Some may not want to mention it ever again. The victim should decide.

Family members can offer to listen whenever she/he wants to talk. Because the victim is in the process of becoming a survivor, she/he may not want to be reminded every day of her/his victimization by a well-meaning family member. However, family denial is also not helpful. Sometimes a family will make an unspoken agreement not to mention the rape so as not to upset the victim. In this case, the victim feels isolated and shut out, unable to share her/his thoughts and feelings when they do arise. Flexibility is the best guide. The family should try to adapt to the changing needs of the victim, encouraging her/him to set the limits for family discussion. Families can be an invaluable resource to a victim of rape if they are able and willing to listen and respond in the midst of this crisis.

Notes

1. Ann Wolbert Burgess and Lynda Lytle Holmstrom, *Rape: Victims of Crisis* (Bowie, Md.: Robert J. Brady Co., 1974), pp. 4, 6.

2. "Rape trauma syndrome is the acute phase and long-term reorganization process that occurs as a result of a forcible rape or attempted forcible rape. This syndrome of behavioral, somatic, and psychological reactions is an acute stress reaction to a life-threatening situation." Ann Wolbert Burgess and Lynda Lytle Holmstrom, "Rape Trauma Syndrome," *The*

American Journal of Psychiatry, 131:9 (September 1974), p. 982. The discussion of Rape Trauma Syndrome reflects primarily the experience of women victims. The general issues are similar for both female and male victims. Additional information follows discussing the particular needs of male victims. See also Ann Wolbert Burgess and Lynda Lytle Holmstrom, *Rape: Victims of Crisis* (Bowie, Md.: Robert J. Brady Co., 1974).

3. A. Nicholas Groth with H. Jean Birnbaum, *Men Who Rape* (New York: Plenum Press, 1979), p. 139.

Chapter 8

RESPONDING TO CHILD SEXUAL ABUSE

AT FIRST HE WOULD JUST STAND BY THE BED AND TOUCH ME. LATER HE BEGAN TO LAY IN THE BED BESIDE ME. ALTHOUGH HE BEGAN BY BEING GENTLE, AS TIME WENT ON, HIS TOUCH BECAME ROUGHER AND ROUGHER. HE WOULD LEAVE ME FEELING SORE AND BRUISED FOR DAYS. IT WAS AS IF HE COMPLETELY LOST TOUCH WITH THE FACT THAT I WAS A CHILD. HE WAS A BULLY WHO PHYSICALLY DOMINATED EVERYONE IN OUR FAMILY. I SAW AND HEARD HIM BEAT UP MY MOTHER SO MANY TIMES THAT I WAS IN CONSTANT FEAR THAT HE WOULD KILL HER. I KNEW THAT I WAS NO MATCH FOR HIM, AND I GUESS I BELIEVED THAT HIS SEXUAL ABUSE WAS SOMEHOW BETTER THAN THE PHYSICAL ABUSE MY MOTHER RECEIVED. TOTAL DETACHMENT BECAME MY WAY OF DEALING WITH WHAT WENT ON AT NIGHT. I WOULD ROLL INTO THE WALL WHEN HE CAME IN, PRETENDING TO BE ASLEEP, TRYING TO BE PART OF THE WALL. I WOULD CRY HYSTERICALLY IN ORDER TO GET SO FAR INTO MY OWN PAIN THAT I WOULDN'T NOTICE WHAT HE WAS DOING. WITH THE PILLOW OVER MY FACE, I TAUGHT MYSELF TO DETACH MY MIND FROM MY BODY. I COULD ACTUALLY SEE MYSELF FROM THE FAR UPPER CORNER OF THE ROOM; I SAW THE LITTLE GIRL CRYING IN BED AND FELT SORRY FOR HER.[1]

AND THEY WERE BRINGING CHILDREN TO HIM, THAT HE MIGHT TOUCH THEM; AND THE DISCIPLES REBUKED THEM. BUT WHEN JESUS SAW IT HE WAS INDIGNANT, AND SAID TO THEM, "LET THE CHILDREN COME TO ME, DO NOT HINDER THEM; FOR TO SUCH BELONGS THE KINGDOM OF GOD. TRULY, I SAY TO YOU, WHOEVER DOES NOT RECEIVE THE KINGDOM OF GOD LIKE A

CHILD SHALL NOT ENTER IT." AND HE TOOK THEM IN
HIS ARMS AND BLESSED THEM, LAYING HIS HANDS UPON
THEM.

Mark 10: 13–16

As with rape, an effective pastoral response to child sexual abuse requires an understanding of the problem and its consequences to victims. Child sexual abuse is perhaps the most disturbing manifestation of sexual violence. Many people have a difficult time imagining that an adult could willfully exploit a child sexually, especially an adult related to a child. As a result, this common childhood experience is frequently overlooked. Freud was so dismayed by the frequency with which his clients reported sexual abuse as children that, rather than face the reality that they expressed, he decided that it was largely fantasy. From this erroneous and unscientific conclusion, Freud developed his theories of female sexual fantasy. His conclusion that the reports from his female clients of sexual abuse by fathers were untrue provided a pseudoscientific basis for the collective denial that children are sexually abused in their families.[2] No one wants to admit the reality of child sexual abuse, so eyes and ears are closed to its victims who seek help. If no one "sees" it, then it does not exist.

Statistics state otherwise: Thirty-eight percent of females and one in ten males will be sexually molested by age 18 years.[3] At least fifty percent of all child sexual abuse occurs in the family as incestuous abuse.[4] Seventy-five percent of female teenage prostitutes on the street have experienced rape, incest, or molestation earlier in their lives.[5] In the past five years, due to their courage and persistence, finally victims of child sexual abuse have begun to be heard; the widespread nature of this crime against children and its consequences for our society are now being understood.

A child may be molested by a stranger, by someone known to her/him, or by a family member. Each of these situations presents different difficulties for the child.

Molestation by a Stranger

When a child is molested by someone not known to her/him, it is usually treated as a crisis. If the child has been taught about sexual abuse, she/he will more than likely go to a trusted adult for help. The adult's response at this point is critical. If the parent, teacher, family friend, etc. reacts with horror and disbelief, immediately moving into crisis her/himself, the child will become anxious for having "caused" this disruption for the adult. The adult's crisis then becomes the focus of responses by friends and others trying to help. An alternative response by an adult to a child's disclosure of sexual abuse is to listen carefully and calmly. Reassure the child that she/he did the right thing in coming to tell you. Repeat that it was not the child's fault. Be clear that you will take care of the situation; you will protect the child. Then call the police and report the incident; call the local rape crisis center and ask for their help as well.

If the offender who abused the child did not use physical force, quick and calm intervention by an adult will insure minimal trauma for the child. The child will ordinarily recover quickly from this unpleasant experience. If the offender used force, the recovery is more difficult for the child because the experience itself was more frightening and traumatic. In either case, a calm, sensitive response is most helpful.

Sexual Abuse by Someone Known

Ninety percent of the time the child victim of sexual abuse will know the offender and chances are high that the offender will be a family member.[6] Sexual abuse by someone known to the child is less likely to be reported by the child and, if unreported, will become a chronic pattern of abuse which may last for years before being revealed. The abuse usually begins between ages three and six and if there is no intervention continues into the child's adolescence. Child sexual abuse includes fondling, masturbating the child, oral/genital/anal penetration, or forcing the child to sexually stimulate the adult or older teenager. A child who is being sexually abused by someone they know is not likely to report the abuse for several reasons: the adult (parent) or older teenager (babysitter) is in a position of authority vis-á-vis the child; the child fears being blamed for doing something wrong; the abuser may offer bribes or threaten physical harm; the child may enjoy receiving this special attention even though it is uncomfortable and confusing. Too frequently a child *has* reported the situation to an adult who refused to believe the child. The child then concludes that adults cannot be trusted or expected to help, so the child tries to cope on her/his own.

Child Victims of Incestuous Abuse

The child or teenager who has been sexually abused and exploited by a family member develops specific coping skills and attitudes in order to survive. These include isolation and detachment, a mistrust of adults, the confusion of sex and affection, low self-esteem, and self-destructive behavior.

Victims often withdraw from their peers. Since the victim rarely shares her/his experience with peers, she/he believes that no one else has ever experienced this before; the victim feels isolated from her/his peers. The victim also feels older than her/his peers and more experienced because she/he is sexually active at an early age. Victims often talk about never knowing childhood. In addition, they may detach themselves from the abuse experience, pretending that it is all a dream, that the sexual contact is really with someone else and not with them, etc. Thus they may come across as being emotionally flat and removed from what they describe.

Child victims learn early not to trust adults. A relationship which should be trustworthy and in which an adult is supposed to care for and protect a child is betrayed by child sexual abuse. Some form of coercion is employed overtly or subtly by the adult to force compliance with his sexual demands. Physical size and authority are used to the offender's advantage. When a victim has asked for help from another adult and not been believed, she/he readily concludes that adults in general cannot be trusted.

Children need emotional and physical affection. Child victims learn that the only affection they are likely to get from the offender is sexual. They also learn that this sexual attention is not for their benefit, but is solely for the benefit of the offender. Hence, they feel exploited. They begin to believe that the only way to get affection is through sex and that sex is basically exploitative and something over which they have no control.

Invariably, child victims lose almost all sense of self-worth. They feel responsible for the sexual abuse and develop overwhelmingly negative feelings about themselves. Their only sense of personal worth comes from being the object of an adult's sexual attention. They quickly begin to think that this is all they are good for.

Sometimes this loss of self-worth moves the child or teenage victim to self-destructive behavior. Drug or alcohol abuse, self-mutilation, overeating, undereating, and suicide attempts may result. These should all be regarded as severe symptoms of a problem and an attempt should be made to discover what lies behind it.

> I believe that children engage in violent and/or self-destructive behavior for a reason. I believe that when children have pain which is hard to express, they will

sometimes do destructive things to themselves and to others in order to be heard. I believe every victim of incest and childhood sexual abuse tried to tell someone, either verbally or by behavior, that something was wrong. We are all so uncomfortable with destructive behavior that we often cannot see beyond it. We deal with the outward, visible signs of feelings because they are more concrete and easier for us to manage than the secret pain or fear that may lie beneath them. As a result, it is often a child's behavior that we confront, rather than what a child is really trying to say. We must learn to do more than just see the behavior or treat the symptoms of incest. We must learn to hear the pain and offer new survival skills.[7]

Frequently we have responded to juvenile deliquent behavior in a judgmental and punitive manner without stopping to assess the source of this behavior. In many cases we have punished juveniles who are themselves victims of the adult behavior we did not want to know about, rather than attending to their needs as victims.

Disclosure

Disclosure of sexual abuse is often frightening and difficult for the child victim. She/he fears not being believed or being punished for lying. Most of all the child fears that no one will do anything to stop the abuse and she/he will face retribution at the hands of the offender. Furthermore, small children often do not have the vocabulary to explain to an adult what is going on and so will use words or images adults do not understand and may easily disregard. For example: A 14-year-old girl brought a girlfriend home from school one afternoon. As they walked into the kitchen, the new friend was introduced to the girl's mother, and immediately the girl's 6-year-old brother ran up to the friend, grabbed her by the legs and said,

"George sucks dicks." He then ran and hid in the hall closet.
The mother and daughter were appalled and embarrassed by
the 6-year-old's behavior. The mother went to find him and
reprimand him. He was sitting in the corner of the closet
crying and looking up at his mother and said, "Mommie, it's
true, it's true."

This 6-year-old boy had been sexually abused by a 15-year-
old neighbor for the past year. He had been afraid to tell
anyone in his family because he feared their disbelief and
rejection, so he chose to tell a perfect stranger in hopes she
would help him. If she rejected him, it would not be as painful for him as rejection by a family member. Children's un-
conventional ways of communicating distress need to be taken
seriously, especially if they have not been provided with vocabulary and concepts which they can use to tell adults about
abuse.

Children may not tell directly, but significant changes in
the child's behavior may be signals which should not be ignored. For example:

- a shift from outgoing behavior to shy, withdrawn behavior (or vice versa);
- regressive behaviors such as resuming thumbsucking
  or bedwetting;
- discomfort or fear of being left alone with a particular
  adult or teenager;
- precocious, provocative sexual behavior, such as imita-
  tion of adult sex play (a child will not act out sexually
  unless she/he has been taught to do so by sexual contact with an adult);
- running away or drug and alcohol abuse;
- nightmares or sleep disturbances.

Any of these indicators should encourage an adult to explore
with the child in a nonaccusatory, sensitive way what has
been happening to her/him.

As adults, we are tempted to ignore or punish children's
distress stories or indications because we really do not want to

know about child sexual abuse. "Recognition of sexual molestation in a child is entirely dependent on the individual's
inherent willingness to entertain the possibility that the condition may exist."[8] If we refuse to believe that it can happen,
then we will not see it when it does happen and we will
conclude that children lie about these things. *Children do not
lie about sexual abuse.* They do not have the details to make
up stories unless they have had the experience. The most
important thing that we can do when we suspect any abuse is
to believe the child and act quickly to intervene.[9]

A report to the police or the state children's protection
office should bring an immediate response. This is important
especially in cases of incestuous abuse because once the family is aware that the child has told the family secret, the family
will close ranks to defend itself from outside intervention. The
abuser will deny the sexual abuse and the child will be pres-
sured to change her/his story. The child may be removed
temporarily from the home by authorities for her/his protection until a decision can be made about what to do. This will
be difficult for a child because it will seem that she/he is
being punished by being sent away. The child may begin to
regret having told.

During this crisis period, agencies can provide crisis intervention and support for the child victim and nonoffending
parent(s). The parent and child need each other for support as
well in order to follow through on prosecution of the offender
so that he/she will get help. Even though the child will be
relieved that someone is helping and that the abuse will stop,
she/he will often be ambivalent because she/he may have
feelings of love and family loyalty for the abuser. The child
may feel guilty and responsible for "breaking up the family."
In addition, the nonoffending parent may feel resentment and
direct that at the child. Those who intervene need to be
sensitive to ambivalence which may be expressed, and see it
as ambivalence rather than as an indicator that the child's
story is false.

NonOffending Parent(s) in Incest Situations

Many people believe that nonoffending parent(s), especially mothers, must have known about the child sexual abuse in their family and thus must have colluded with the offender. For example, they wonder how a mother could not know that her child was being sexually abused by the father or father figure in the home. While some mothers may have known, most mothers of incest victims do not know about the abuse. After disclosure of the abuse, they may look back and realize that the child was giving them clues, for example, asking not to be left home alone with her father. At the time, however, the mother may never even have considered the possibility of incest. When faced with the child's disclosure, the mother is then confronted with the difficult choice of whom to believe, her child or her husband. Sometimes a mother will choose to believe the husband, largely because she cannot handle the ramifications of believing the child. But often, with support, she is able to face the reality that her husband is sexually abusing her child and to take the steps necessary to protect the children.

The mother is in a difficult situation. She may be horrified at the thought that her husband could do such a thing to the children, and yet feel emotionally and economically dependent on him and fearful that she cannot survive if she forces him to leave the home. She may be a battered wife and afraid of his violence toward her if she tries to stop his abuse of the children.[10] The mother may have a strained relationship with her child (especially a teenager) who has been acting out for several years or whom she feels in competition with for her husband's attention. This will make it difficult for her to believe and support her child. In her confusion and crisis, she may blame the child for causing this upheaval and jeopardizing the family's future.

Because the nonoffending parents are the primary resource for the child victim after disclosure of the abuse, anything that a pastor, counselor, friend, or family member can do to support them and encourage support of their child is valuable. Nonoffending parents are in crisis too; they may not be making reasonable decisions or behaving responsibly; they need help in understanding what has happened and what options are available. Their feelings and confusion are as important as the victim's and must be addressed. A mother may think about separation or divorce, feeling that she cannot live with a person who would abuse her children. There are religious considerations for most women who are contemplating divorce. She may choose to prosecute the offender in order to get him into treatment and then wait to decide about divorce until after he completes treatment. She needs support so that she can support her child.[11]

Adult Women Who Were Victims as Children[12]

As the topic of incest becomes more openly discussed, more adult women are beginning to acknowledge and discuss their experiences as child victims of sexual abuse in their families. These victims may be realizing for the first time that they are not alone in their experiences and, by talking with other women who were also victims, begin to resolve some of the feelings they have carried for years. A support group for adult women who were child victims of incest is an ideal place to deal with these experiences.

Because she believes that she is the only person whose father (or other family member) was sexual with her, an adult incest victim has sustained her isolation from other people for years. Believing that she carries a secret that no one could comprehend, a victim may maintain a "safe" emotional distance from everyone. Depression and self-destructive behavior may be ongoing problems for adult women who were victims as children.

Anger is a common feeling expressed by adult victims of incest. This anger which may have lain under the surface for years, eventually comes out. The anger may be directed at themselves for not being able to stop the abuse or protect their younger siblings from abuse, at their mother for not protecting them, or at the offender. Victims at this point should be encouraged to identify and express their anger, and direct it most appropriately toward the offender, the source of the abuse. (See Chapter 10, "Religious Concerns and Pastoral Issues.")

Because for many victims there was no intervention or assistance for them as children, as adults they have a strong sense of unfinished business. The victim's anger, guilt, and confusion are unresolved. The adult victim may choose to act on her own behalf at this point by confronting the offender. This can be done in person or by letter. Letters written expressing the victim's pain and anger may never be mailed and yet still be effective. If the offender is dead, the opportunity for confrontation is not there, but writing such a letter can be a valuable step for the victim anyway. It is important to remember that a victim's desire to confront the offender always carries with it the expectation that the offender will acknowledge his offense and ask for forgiveness, preparing the way for some form of reconciliation. In fact, the offender may well continue to deny that the abuse ever took place and may be unwilling to discuss the matter at all. A victim should be prepared for this disappointment. Nonetheless, she has done what she needed to do in confronting his abuse toward her.

Some victims of incest experience sexual difficulties as adults. They feel fearful of sexual contact with a partner or simply separate their emotions from sexual activity (as they did when they were children). Sexual dysfunction may also be a problem. Adults who were victims may avoid sexual relationships altogether or may engage in frequent and indiscriminate sexual activity. Most sexual problems which face adult victims are related to their fear of intimacy (emotional, sexual, etc.) which comes from their childhood experience of betrayal in an intimate, family relationship. Intimacy requires risk and vulnerability, both of which may be very difficult for adults who were incest victims. Having been sexually exploited in one's family, it is not easy to trust someone again enough to be truly intimate with them. Incest victims who, as adults, have taken the opportunity to discuss their experiences and feelings with other victims or with a trained counselor, have found this a helpful means of breaking out of their isolation and beginning the healing process. Incestuous abuse experienced as a child need not diminish one's relationships with others in adult life.

Notes

1. Barbara Myers, "Developmental Disruptions of Victims of Incest and Childhood Abuse," (1978), Mimeographed paper, p. 5.
2. Florence Rush has provided a valuable discussion of the "Freudian Cover-up" in *The Best Kept Secret: Sexual Abuse of Children* (Englewood Cliffs, N.J.: Prentice-Hall, 1980), pp. 80 f. In this chapter, she quotes Freud's conclusions: "Almost all of my women patients told me that they had been seduced by their fathers. I was driven to recognize in the end that these reports were untrue and so came to understand that the hysterical symptoms are derived from phantasies and not real occurences."
3. Diana E. H. Russell, "The Incidence and Prevalence of Intrafamilial and Extrafamilial Sexual Abuse of Female Children," *Child Abuse and Neglect: The International Journal* (October 1982), p. 1 of mimeographed copy. Figures for male child victims are also significant: 1 in 10 male children will be sexually abused by age 18 years according to 1981 statistics from the Sexual Assault Center, Harborview Medical Center, Seattle, Washington.
4. Statistics from 1979 report prepared by the Sexual Assault Center, Harborview Medical Center, Seattle, Washington.
5. Jennifer James, Principal Investigator, and Debra Boyer, "Entrance into Juvenile Prostitution," August, 1980. Research

supported by National Institute of Mental Health grant MH 29968, 1980. The figure for male teenage prostitutes is even higher at 83% having been sexually abused in early life. Jennifer James, Principal Investigator, and Debra Boyer, "Entrance into Juvenile Male Prostitution," August, 1982; Research supported by National Institute of Mental Health grant RO1MH 29968, 1982. For further information, James and Boyer can be contacted through the Department of Anthropology, University of Washington, Seattle, Washington.

6. Sexual Assault Center.

7. Myers, p. 1.

8. Dr. Suzanne M. Sgroi, in "Sexual Abuse of Children," Sexual Assault Center, 1977.

9. In the rare event that a child is lying, it will become apparent immediately and can be dealt with.

10. We are seeing an increasingly high correlation between spouse abuse and incestuous abuse.

11. Groups for mothers of incest victims are an excellent means of helping them rally resources and get support from others in the same situation. These groups are offered by some rape or sexual assault agencies in local communities.

12. As the title of this section indicates, it is limited to female victims. It is apparent that some men who were child incest victims grow up to become sex offenders. See Chapter 9, "Responding to Sex Offenders." Data on male victims who do not become offenders is limited at this time and so I have not attempted to discuss this here.

RESPONDING TO SEX OFFENDERS

> THE SEXUAL OFFENDER MAY BE PASSIVE AND INHIBITED OR ACTIVE AND ASSERTIVE, GENTLE OR VIOLENT, RELIGIOUS OR IRRELIGIOUS, MASCULINE OR EFFEMINATE. HE MAY HATE HIS MOTHER, LOVE HIS MOTHER, OR BE AMBIVALENT ABOUT HER. HE MAY HAVE HAD A REPRESSIVE SEXUAL DEVELOPMENT OR HE MAY HAVE BEEN OVERSTIMULATED. AND WE COULD GO ON WITH THESE POLAR OPPOSITES. BUT WHAT THERE IS IN COMMON IS A SERIOUS DEFECT IN THE INTERPERSONAL RELATIONSHIPS, AN ABSENCE OF MATURE, SELFLESS CONCERN FOR THE VICTIM OF HIS OBSESSION, AN INABILITY TO LOVE IN A DESEXUALIZED MANNER, A TERRIBLE SADNESS AND SENSE OF LONELINESS, A LACK OF SUBLIMATION, AND A TOTALLY NARCISSISTIC, SELF-CENTERED ORIENTATION.
>
> Dr. Murray L. Cohen and Richard Boucher in "Misunderstandings About Sex Criminals," *Sexual Behavior,* as quoted in Nancy Gager and Cathleen Schurr, *Sexual Assault: Confronting Rape in America*

The current stereotypes of the rapist range from the traditional image of a dirty, sleazy, sex-starved crazy man to a contemporary image of Everyman.[1] The fact is that the latter comes closer to the truth. It now appears that rapists differ from so-called "normal" men only in that they tend to be more aggressive. In all other respects, their characteristics and lifestyles are not unlike the rest of the male population.

This chapter will provide a brief overview of the sex of-

176

fender along with suggestions for appropriate responses if a clergy or lay counselor should encounter a rapist or child molester. It is in no way intended to be an exhaustive discussion. The work of Nicholas Groth and J. Birnbaum as presented in *Men Who Rape* provides the basis for most of the following information. This book is suggested as a resource for those seeking additional material.

Rapists

In understanding the behavior of the rapist, it is important to remember that rape is a pseudosexual act. Rape "is in fact serving primarily nonsexual needs. It is the sexual expression of power and anger."[2] The rapist does not rape because he is oversexed or has no sexual outlet. In fact, the majority of rapists are sexually active with their wives or other sexual partners during the period when they rape. While most rapists are not insane (insanity implying being out of control of their behavior), the rape is a symptom of serious psychological dysfunction. "The rapist is, in fact, a person who has serious psychological difficulties which handicap him in his relationships to other people and which he discharges, when he is under stress, through sexual acting-out."[3] He is limited in his ability to exhibit trust, empathy, compassion, and sensitivity and his relationships lack intimacy, emotion, mutuality, and openness. He has distorted and/or negative views of his victim and thus often sees her as available and "wanting to be raped" or "getting what she deserved." He tends to be sexually uninformed and insecure.

"Rape is always and foremost an aggressive act."[4] This aggression, which is expressed through sexual contact, involves hostility, resentment, anger, and frustration in various complex combinations. The three basic patterns of rape provide a means of understanding the different types of rapists: the power rape, the anger rape, and the sadistic rape.

POWER RAPE[5]

The power rapist wants to possess, control, and dominate his victim; his goal is sexual conquest. Physical force is used only as necessary to achieve the victim's sexual submission. His sexual *fantasies* focus on rape and conquest: "The victim [in his fantasy] initially resists the sexual advances of her assailant; he overpowers her and achieves sexual penetration; in spite of herself, the victim cannot resist her assailant's sexual prowess and becomes sexually aroused and receptive to his embrace."[6] But the rapist reports little sexual satisfaction from the actual assault; it is a disappointment and never quite lives up to his fantasy. Clearly this rapist is not looking for consensual sex. He is seeking to reaffirm his masculinity about which he feels insecure. Power rapists tend to be homophobic, and rape as a way of asserting their heterosexuality, reassuring themselves that they are not in any way homosexual. For them, all types of sexual expression are threatening and produce insecure feelings. In seeking proof of their virility, they deny that the sexual contact was forced. They tell themselves that their victims really did want and enjoy it. Afterward they may treat them gently and politely, believing that they have created in their victims a desire for them.

ANGER RAPE[7]

The anger rapist is usually forceful and brutal and literally attacks his victims. He expresses his rage physically and verbally. He seeks to humiliate and harm his victim. Using sex as a weapon, he rapes as the "ultimate offense." The anger rapist does not find sexual satisfaction in the rape experience, and may in fact be impotent during the assault. Usually this rape is precipitated by some specific stress in the rapist's life, e.g., a dispute, conflict, or aggravation. He commonly feels that he has been wronged or put down and seeks revenge, often against women, for what he perceives to be wrongs they committed against him. The victim may be the actual object of the rapist's anger or a substitute. His rapes are sporadic and infrequent, occuring when his anger and frustration reach a volatile point.

SADISTIC RAPE[8]

In sadistic rape, there is a more direct link between sexuality and aggression. The aggression has become eroticized, i.e, the rapist finds sexual gratification in tormenting and abusing the victim. Bondage and torture are frequently employed, and the assault may finally result in homicide. He may find the resistance of his victim to be sexually exciting. Sadomasochistic, sexually explicit materials are utilized by the sadistic rapist. His sadistic impulses may also appear in consensual sexual encounters or in nonsexual situations, like cruelty to animals.

The amount of public and media attention given to sadistic rape is disproportionate to its incidence. Unfortunately, this gives an unrealistic picture of what rape is by focusing on the bizarre and unusual and by overlooking the more common forms of rape. As a result, people's efforts at protection and prevention are often skewed and do not take into account the type of rape most likely to occur, i.e., power or anger rapes. Consequently, people are less likely to be prepared for an attempted sexual assault by a power or anger rapist, e.g., by a friend, acquaintance, or family member.

While these categories provide a way of understanding the differences in motivation among rapists, they are also very neat and clear cut, which can lead the reader to the erroneous belief that rapists can be clearly identified and categorized on this basis. In fact, rapists are generally indistinguishable from other men. This is partly indicative of the blurred distinction between "normal" male sexuality and rape behavior. "Power rape," to use Groth's term, describes coercive sexual activity which is regarded by some as "normal" behavior. The sex offenders most likely to be encountered by a pastor or counselor will probably not fit neatly into a category. They probably won't see their own behavior as a sexual offense. Even though the offender's behavior may not fit into one of these three categories, pastors and counselors are cautioned not to minimize any indications of coercive or assaultive sexual behavior.

Same Sex Rape

The men who rape other men do not differ greatly from the men who rape women. In fact, for approximately half of those who rape men, the gender of the victim does not seem to matter a great deal: They rape either men or women. The others seek out males specifically and for the same reason that men rape women: to control, dominate, humiliate, and abuse another person.

Descriptively, men who rape men present a wide range of sexual orientation in their experiences of consenting sexual activity. Of those studied by Groth and Birnbaum, twenty-six percent would be described as bisexual and only seven percent as homosexual.[9] However, Groth and Birnbaum rightly point out that

> To define the sexual lifestyle of these offenders as heterosexual or homosexual is not actually an accurate description of their sexual orientation, since in general, their interpersonal relationships lacked such qualities as empathy, mutuality, and reciprocity. Instead, with one or two exceptions, they tended to possess a rather ambiguous and undefined sexuality that was more self-centered than interpersonal. Their relationships to others, both sexual and nonsexual, were based more on exploitation than sharing.[10]

It appears that for these men, homophobia may be a significant factor in their choice of a male victim.

The selection of a male as the target of their sexual assault can in part be seen as an expression of this unresolved aspect of their lives. The victim may symbolize what they want to control, punish, and/or destroy—something they want to conquer and defeat. The assault is an act of retaliation, an expression of power, and an assertion of their strength or manhood.[11]

Since rapists find satisfaction in the domination of another person, for some it is even more satisfying to subdue a male than a female because in doing so, they symbolically emasculate the male and make a victim of one who is not *supposed* to be a victim.

In the prison setting, the rape of men by men represents the same things that rape in the community does (e.g., acting out of aggression, anger, sadism). In addition, it helps establish and maintain a social hierarchy in which inmates make it very clear who has power over the others.

When a person feels powerless in regard to controlling his life, he can defend against the discomfort of such an experience by asserting control over someone else. In this way, he comes to feel more powerful than his victim and thus compensates for his feelings of inadequacy. This is particularly evident in prison rape, where the offender's tenuous sense of identity, personal control, and self-esteem are further diminished by his incarceration. Sexual assault becomes a means of compensating for his sense of helplessness and vulnerability and of retaliating for his feelings of resentment and anger.[12]

Thus, the prison setting becomes a closed system, a microcosm of the dynamics of sexual assault in the larger society.

Child Molesters

Contrary to popular opinion, the child molester is a relatively young, heterosexual man who is neither insane, nor retarded, nor sexually frustrated. He seeks to control the child more than to injure him/her and most of the time poses more of a psychological than a physical risk to the victim. His behavior is highly repetitive, often to the point of a compulsion, rather than being the result of a temporary lapse of judgment while in a state of intoxication. His crime is a symptom and imprisonment alone is insufficient to remedy the underlying causes for his problem behavior.[13]

Child molesters or pedophiles (i.e., child lovers) can be classified according to their pattern of molesting as either fixated or regressed. Some child molesters (fixated) have from an early age been sexually attracted to persons younger than themselves. They avoid relationships with adults, fearing rejection. They find children less demanding than adults and more likely to be accepting of them as persons. They experience no sense of regret or of the inappropriateness of their behavior with children. Other child molesters (regressed) preferred adult sexual partners until their adult relationships began to present difficulties and conflicts. Faced with this stress, they turned their attention to children. They feel inadequate to deal with adult responsibilities and so retreat and use children as an emotional and sexual outlet.[14]

The child molester gains sexual access to a child in one of two ways. He may *pressure* the child by offering a reward, telling the child that all girls or boys do this, offering instruction ("Let me teach you a new game."), etc. The offender wants approval and affection from the child, and so seeks out a cooperative victim. Any resistance on the child's part will often discourage him. Other child molesters will use *verbal or physical force* to gain access to the child. A child's resistance in this situation is not likely to be effective.[15] In any child molesting situation, the offender uses his position of authority, power, or physical strength to take advantage of a child's vulnerability.

The child molester is usually known to his victim.[16] He may be a family member, family friend, neighbor, babysitter, teacher, pastor, etc. The molester who is known to his victim also takes advantage of whatever trust relationship may have developed between them.

The vast majority of child molesters (whether they offend against males or females) identify themselves as heterosexual. Occasionally, they are bisexual and rarely they are homosexual. The all-too-common belief that most child molesters are homosexuals "recruiting" young children has no basis in fact.[17] Offenders who approach young boys indicate that they are attracted by the boy's feminine characteristics, i.e., the absence of secondary sex characteristics like body hair, and are repulsed by the thought of sexual contact with an adult male.[18] "It appears, then that the heterosexual adult constitutes more of a threat of sexual victimization to the underage child than does the homosexual adult."[19] Thus, in an effort to protect children effectively from child molesters, attention should be focused on heterosexuals or homosexuals *who are offenders*, rather than on homosexuals as a group, who are least likely to be offenders.

Incest Offenders

Incestuous assault represents at least fifty percent of the sexual abuse of children by someone they know.[20] In this case, the offender is a family member: usually father or stepfather, and sometimes uncle, grandfather, brother, live-in boyfriend, or foster parent. In less than one percent of reported cases, the offender is a female relative.[21] The incest offender may fit any of the categories of child molester previously discussed. Child sexual abuse within the family may be a part of a pattern of family violence which may also include other forms of child abuse or spouse abuse by the offender. His feelings of inadequacy, low self-esteem, and isolation, coupled with poor impulse control and ready access to children in the family create a potentially abusive situation. The incest offender is often a very rigid and authoritarian person who espouses a strict moral code, especially in regard to sexual matters. Somehow he accommodates his moral code in his pattern of sexual abuse of children. While he would never seek out a prostitute, he does not question the morality or appropriateness of using his child as a sexual outlet. He prefers to "keep it in the family."

Sex Offenders' History of Sexual Trauma

While the factors which lead a person to become a rapist or child molester are complex and multidimensional, one aspect which deserves attention is the offender's experience of abuse in his own development. A majority of sex offenders experienced physical and/or sexual abuse as children,[22] most frequently by someone known to them. These early experiences, in which there was probably no intervention or assistance for the child victim, contribute significantly to poor self-image, lack of trust in relationships, and anger. Groth concludes:

> The offender's adult crimes may be in part a repetition and an acting out of a sexual offense he was subjected to as a child, a maladaptive effort to solve an unresolved early sexual trauma. It can be observed especially with reference to the child molester, that his later offenses often appear to duplicate the aspects of his own victimization, that is age of victim, type of acts performed, and the like . . . Although the complex social problem of sexual assault cannot be reduced to merely the result and perpetuation of early sexual trauma, the sexual assault of children and adolescents poses an issue that should not be ignored and underscores the need for intervention services to prevent any long-range after effects, whether these be sexual dysfunction, sexual aversion, sexual aggression, or other nonsexual problems.[23]

Understanding that some aspects of the offender's own early experiences may contribute to his assaultive behavior in no way excuses his attacks, but it can enable more effective rehabilitation which finally benefits all members of society. It also clearly points to the need to provide effective intervention and counseling services for both male and female victims of child sexual abuse. This is one way to begin to break the cycle of abusive behavior which seems to be so easily passed from generation to generation. (See Chapter 8, "Responding to Child Sexual Abuse.")

The Teenage Offender

The teenage sex offender represents a significant proportion of all offenders, yet his offense is often overlooked or disregarded because "boys will be boys." In fact, sexually assaultive behavior for a teenage male is often a prelude to adult sexual offenses. Only a small percentage of teenage offenders are female. A teenage offender may assault a peer, an adult, or abuse a younger child; his/her behavior may be violent and aggressive or coercive and manipulative. Frequently the teenager will sexually abuse someone known to him/her, e.g., a younger sibling. Another common situation is the case of a teenage babysitter who has responsibility for younger children and takes advantage of them.

Many factors contribute to the high incidence of teenage offenders. Adolescence compounds the teenage offender's problems, bringing alienation and difficulty in social adjustment. Destructive family relationships provide negative models. Lack of accurate information about sexuality limits healthy sexual development. Media images which promote the confusion between sexuality and violence contribute to the teenager's confusion about his own experience. A high rate of actual abuse (emotional, physical, and sexual) of teenagers throughout their growing up creates negative self-images and distrust of others. All of these factors can result in a teenager who sexually offends against others, and who, without intervention, will most likely continue to offend as he/she becomes an adult.

Intervention with Offenders

Pastors or counselors may find themselves in a situation requiring early intervention with a sex offender, either because of specific information shared by the offender himself, e.g., in a confessional context, because the offender has been arrested, or because someone else in the family has sought help, e.g., an incest victim. In any of these cases, the pastor or counselor needs to be aware of several factors as he/she responds to the offender.

- Sex offenders seldom tell the truth about their behavior. They will minimize, deny, and lie about what happened. This is especially true for child molesters: "Nothing really happened. . . ," "I was just giving him a bath. . . ." "Don't believe that kid; she lies all the time. . . ," "I was drunk; I don't remember a thing . . ."
- Sex offenders seldom express remorse or any sense that what they did was wrong.
- Sex offenders will be most concerned with the consequences facing them once they are caught. In this regard, they can be very manipulative of those around them and may well try to mobilize a minister's support as a character witness in their behalf.
- Sex offenders are repeat offenders and will continue to assault and abuse others until they are stopped. Experience indicates that the legal system often provides the leverage needed to get an offender into a treatment program and keep him there as long as necessary. Or, if treatment is not advised, then incarceration will at least protect the community from the offender.

The pastor's or counselor's role at this point is a significant one; he/she can be an important link in the confrontation of the offender's assault. In conjunction with family members and legal and medical authorities, the pastor or counselor can provide the offender with the consistent message that what he has done is wrong and must stop *and* that help is available.

A man came into his pastor's office looking for help. He told his pastor that he had been "messing around" with his 9-year-old daughter. In response to the pastor's questions, the man admitted that he had finally decided that this was wrong and he wanted to know if God and the pastor could forgive him. The pastor replied, "John, you know that God forgives those who are truly sorry for their sins, and I can certainly forgive you. We are going to pray about this right now together and ask God's forgiveness and as soon as we finish, we are going to call up a psychologist I know and get you into treatment."

This was not quite the response that the incest offender was looking for. He was mostly interested in some quick forgiveness and reassurance that everything would be all right. He had not bargained for a pastor who knew that, in addition to spiritual counsel, he needed treatment to make sure that he did not molest his daughter again. John did go into treatment and the pastor arranged to meet with him once a week for prayer and Bible study. In this way, the pastor was able to monitor John's involvement in treatment and to offer the encouragement and support that he needed for the long process of rehabilitation.

The minister or counselor needs to be able to confront the offender and not become a partner in minimizing what he/she is doing. In addition, he/she should offer support throughout the treatment process. The minister or counselor should not expect to be a primary therapist for a sex offender who needs a specially designed treatment program.

Successful treatment of sex offenders is extremely difficult because the state-of-the-art is limited. Treatment of rapists focuses on the offender's violence and aggression, low self-image, covert fantasizing, and possibly unresolved childhood victimization. Working with child molesters is even more difficult in some ways because in contrast with most rapists, the offender does derive significant sexual gratification from his offense which reinforces the behavior. It is clear with these offenders that insight, confession, and remorse are not sufficient to change their behavior. Long-term behavior-oriented treatment is required.

A number of treatment programs for sex offenders are now available in the United States. Programs for rapists are usually connected to a prison or inpatient mental health facility. Child molesters are most often treated in outpatient community-based programs or by private therapists. Treatment philosophies and approaches differ from program to program and have varying degrees of success. The first goal of any program should be the safety of the community (particularly the safety of the child in an incestuous abuse situation) and second, the effective treatment of the offender so that the offender does not repeat his/her assaultive behavior. For the incest offender, this may well mean being separated from the family during treatment. This is the only way to insure the protection of the child victim from further abuse.

Some people advocate imprisonment for all sex offenders; others support capital punishment as the solution. They argue that treatment somehow excuses the offender and may allow him/her to repeat the offense. In fact, imprisonment of rapists, while it may be necessary at some point for the protection of society, does not rehabilitate them but gives them more embittering experiences that feed their desire to sexually assault others. As Groth points out, ". . . incarceration may be necessary, but, in and of itself, it is insufficient to reduce recidivism."[24] For those who are treatable, effective treatment programs are a must. For those who are not treatable, imprisonment, with all its limitations and imperfections, remains the only option. Both represent a stopgap means of dealing with the symptom—the rapist's violent behavior—of a deeply rooted social problem.

Notes

1. See Nancy Gager and Cathleen Schurr, *Sexual Assault: Confronting Rape in America* (New York: Grosset and Dunlap, 1976), p. 205.
2. A. Nicholas Groth with H. Jean Birnbaum, *Men Who Rape* (New York: Plenum Press, 1979), p. 3.
3. *Ibid.*, p. 6.
4. *Ibid.*, p. 12.
5. 55% of those studied by Groth and Birnbaum.
6. Groth with Birnbaum, p. 26.
7. 40% of those studied by Groth and Birnbaum.
8. 5% of those studied by Groth and Birnbaum.
9. Groth with Birnbaum, p. 124.
10. *Ibid.*, p. 125.
11. *Ibid.*, p. 126.
12. *Ibid.*, p. 132.
13. *Ibid.*, p. 151.
14. A. Nicholas Groth, "Patterns of Sexual Assault Against Children and Adolescents," in Ann Wolbert Burgess et al, *Sexual Assault of Children and Adolescents* (Lexington, Ma.: Lexington Books, 1978), pp. 10–11.
15. Groth with Birnbaum, *Men Who Rape*, pp. 142–43.
16. Ninety percent of the time the child molester is known to his victim. Sexual Assault Center, Harborview Medical Center, Seattle, Washington, 1980.
17. "Those offenders who selected underage male victims either have always done so *exclusively* or have regressed from adult *heterosexual* relationships. There were no homosexual, adult-oriented offenders in our sample who turned to children." Groth, *Sexual Assault of Children and Adolescents*, pp. 4–5.
18. Groth with Birnbaum, *Men Who Rape*, p. 149.
19. *Ibid.*, p. 148.
20. Sexual Assault Center, Harborview Medical Center, Seattle, Washington, 1980.

21. *Ibid.*
22. *Ibid.*
23. Groth with Birnbaum, *Men Who Rape,* pp. 102–103.
24. *Ibid.,* p. 109.

Chapter 10
RELIGIOUS CONCERNS AND PASTORAL ISSUES

When in crisis, most people rely on their basic beliefs and values about the world and their place in it. For religious people, these beliefs and values are often principles of faith and/or doctrine. Questions like "Why is this happening to me?" "Why is God doing this to me?" "Am I being punished for my sinfulness?" are common reactions to the experience of sexual assault. For some people, these questions take priority over questions about seeking medical care or calling the police. Because these religious questions are a priority, they must be addressed or they will become obstacles which prevent the victim from dealing with the more practical issues. In addition, the experience of sexual violence may become a crisis of faith for the victim. Since a crisis of faith often is of ultimate importance for a religious person, it may well take precedence over the more practical crisis at hand. In this case, efforts at crisis intervention by helpers will be thwarted until the crisis of faith is acknowledged and addressed.

The following situation presents a graphic example of the way in which a person's religious beliefs and practices can be a major block to dealing with a crisis like sexual violence:

Two rape crisis counselors answered a call from a rape victim and arrived at her home to find her sitting on her sofa reading from the Bible. The counselors ignored the Bible and proceeded to provide crisis intervention; finally, the woman decided to go to the hospital for medical treatment. The counselors and the victim proceeded to the hospital

191

emergency room, the victim reading her Bible all the way. Upon arrival, the three were taken to an examination room and the victim was prepared for her medical exam. She lay on the exam table, feet in stirrups, and continued to read her Bible. When the doctor came in, he noticed her unusual behavior and asked the victim, "Is there something you would like to talk about before I do the exam?" She replied, "Yes, I am a Jehovah's Witness and I am afraid of what my church will do to me when they find out that I have been raped. May I read a few verses from the Bible out loud?" She read from the Bible, closed it, set it aside, and the doctor proceeded with the examination.

Following the examination, it was determined that the victim was at high risk for pregnancy because of the rape. The doctor recommended the morning-after-treatment. The woman knew that she could not take the treatment without permission from her church. So the rape crisis counselors telephoned each of the twelve elders of her congregation in the early hours of the morning to ask their permission. Fortunately, when the situation was explained to them, each was very willing for the woman to have the treatment she needed.

Attention to the victim's religious concerns in the midst of the crisis can help the victim understand her/his experience in light of her/his faith, and thereby enable the victim to utilize faith as a resource. Strengthened and encouraged in their faith, victims are better able to cope with the immediate crisis of the sexual assault. The task for a pastor or counselor is to remove the block which may be created by a victim's religious concerns and allow the individual's spiritual resources to be tapped. The experience of the Jehovah's Witness woman is a good example. As soon as her concerns were acknowledged and affirmed, she was able to proceed with the more practical matters facing her. Her Bible and her faith were then a source of support for her. Asking for and receiving permission from her church for the treatment she needed also allowed her to deal with the practical part of her crisis. Not only was doctrinal permission given, but the affirmative response from the elders was perceived by her as personal support. Thus she then felt encouraged to go to her congregation for support as she recovered from the assault. Her faith and her church became resources to her.

In the midst of the crisis of sexual assault, victims primarily need compassion, support, and sympathy. Like Job, victims need the understanding of friends and family, church and community. Too often, like Job's comforters, those around them misperceive their need. As Kushner points out in *When Bad Things Happen To Good People:*

> What Job needed from his friends—what he was really asking for when he said, "Why is God doing this to me?"—was not theology, but sympathy. He did not really want them to explain God to him, and he certainly did not want them to show him where his theology was faulty. He wanted them to tell him that he was in fact a good person, and that the things that were happening to him were terribly tragic and unfair. But the friends got so bogged down talking about God that they almost forgot about Job, except to tell him that he must have done something pretty awful to deserve this fate at the hands of a righteous God.[1]

This caution is helpful when we encounter someone in the midst of the pain of an assault. The questions and concerns about faith and theology will come soon enough.

Making Sense Out of Experience

In the aftermath of the crisis of sexual violence, one of the most common reactions from victims is to try somehow to understand why the violence happened to them. Many people focus on details as a way to regain a sense of control over the situation. If they can figure out *why* it happened, or what circumstances led to the assault, then they think that they can prevent being victimized again by avoiding those circumstances in the future. On the whole, this effort to understand the "why" of one's victimization is a healthy sign. It is in fact an effort to regain some semblance of control of one's life and environment, i.e., to regain that which was lost in the assault. As discussed earlier (Chapter 7, "Responding to Rape Victims"), it is a step toward recovery and healing and should be encouraged.

In struggling with the question of "why" the assault occurred, victims may seek religious explanations which all too often are inadequate and simplistic. It can be tempting for a rape victim or an incest victim to arrive at an explanation of the experience based on a simple formula which combines self-blame and God-blame. For example:

A 55-year-old woman was raped by a stranger who broke into her home during the night. Her explanation for why this had happened to her was that God was punishing her for having divorced her husband ten years earlier.

A 19-year-old woman had been sexually abused by her older brother since she was 10 years old. Her explanation was that the incestuous abuse was God's punishment for her being a bad person. In addition, at age 15 she had an abortion because she had been impregnated by her brother. The incestuous abuse continued and then she was convinced that God was punishing her for having had the abortion.

A battering husband, in addition to physically beating his wife, also regularly raped her. She interpreted this pattern of abuse as God's way of correcting her tendency to rebel against the authority of her husband.

A gay man who had just begun to be more open about his sexual orientation was kidnapped and brutally raped by three men. He falsely concluded that God was punishing him for his positive feelings about his homosexuality.

All four of these victims see the sexual violence they encountered as God's punishment of them. They justified this by viewing themselves as sinful people who deserve punishment. Self-blame and God-blame together make a simple, yet limited explanation of their suffering that is based more on superstition than on sound theology. Such an explanation once again avoids placing responsibility on the offender.

In these situations, the victims' efforts to comprehend their experiences in light of their religious faith should be affirmed, supported, and nurtured. However, simplistic and superstitious explanations are to be discouraged and challenged by anyone doing pastoral counseling. Unfortunately, the church has often encouraged people to seek these simple answers when in crisis. Too often the church has promised that if a person lives a good, Christian life (i.e., goes to church regularly, prays, reads the Bible, etc.), she/he will never again experience suffering. When people do experience suffering or crisis (as they invariably will), they are faced with two choices: (1) even though they tried to live a Christian life, they must have failed somehow and God is punishing them; or (2) although they were living by the rules they still suffered; so they conclude that the basis of their faith must be bankrupt. In this case, they turn away from their faith in anger. Neither choice adequately explains the experience of suffering. But the church's promise implicitly or explicitly of no more suffering sets people up to face this double bind. Simple answers are inadequate to the complexity of the suffering of sexual violence and cut people off from the resources of their faith.

Why Is There Suffering?

It is important to understand the experience of the suffering of sexual violence in terms of one's religious perspective. To ask the questions from a perspective of faith, "Why do I suffer in this way" and "Where is God in my suffering," is to come to terms with oneself in relation to God and the universe. These are profound theological questions which cannot be simply answered with platitudes and then dismissed. The question of why there is suffering at all is a question of classic theological debate to which there is no completely satisfactory answer. Human suffering in the midst of a world created by a compassionate and loving God is a dimension of human experience which is most disturbing. For the purposes of this discussion, there are two aspects of the experience of suffering with which persons struggle when they ask "Why is there suffering?"

First is the question of cause, i.e., the source of the suffering. For some it suffices to say that suffering is caused by human sinfulness, i.e., sinful acts bring suffering to others. God *allows* such sinfulness because God has given persons free will and does not intervene when persons choose unrighteous acts. People simply live with the consequences of these acts. This explanation may be adequate for situations clearly caused by human negligence or meanness, intended or not, for example, a fatal car accident caused by a drunk driver; chronic brown lung disease in textile workers who are denied protection from occupational hazards; birth defects in families living near chemical dumps; or incestuous abuse inflicted by a father who was himself a victim of child abuse.[2]

For victims of sexual violence, although the inclination is to hold God or oneself responsible, there is clearly a perpetrator whose actions resulted in suffering for the victim. His sinful acts can be understood as a consequence of his own brokenness and alienation (see "Naming the Unmentionable Sin" in Chapter 3).

The second question relating to understanding suffering involves the question of meaning. What meaning does this experience of suffering hold for the victim? An interpretation of the meaning of one's suffering begins with the differentiation between voluntary and involuntary suffering. *Voluntary suffering* is a painful experience which a person chooses in order to accomplish a greater good. For example, the acts of civil disobedience by civil rights workers in the U.S. in the 1960s led to police brutality and imprisonment. These consequences were unjustifiable and should not have been inflicted. Yet people chose to endure this suffering in order to change the circumstances of oppression which caused even greater suffering for many people. Like voluntary suffering, *involuntary suffering* is unjustifiable under any circumstances; it should never happen. However, unlike voluntary suffering, involuntary suffering is not chosen and serves no greater good. Rape and child sexual abuse are forms of involuntary suffering. Neither serves any useful purpose; neither is chosen by the victim; neither should ever happen to anyone. Yet both do happen. And the frequent question in response is: Why did God send *me* this affliction? Frequently responses include: (1) this is God's way of testing my faith, (2) this is God's punishment for my sins, or (3) this is God's way of strengthening my character. To each is added the superficial reassurance that God does not give us a heavier yoke than we can bear. All of these responses imply that God is responsible. Such responses attempt to engender meaning in the suffering itself, e.g., to build character. People have difficulty accepting that such painful experiences as rape and child sexual abuse happen *for no good reason*. So they try to create a "good reason" or seek a "greater good."

In Jesus' encounter with the man born blind (John 9:1–12), he is confronted with the question about the cause and meaning of suffering. He is asked by the people if the man was born blind because of his parents' sin or because of his own.[3] Jesus avoids creating "a good reason" and suggests that the meaning of suffering lies in other questions. Jesus restated the question: Where is God in this suffering and what can God do in this situation?

The theology of the cross and resurrection provides insight to the meaning of suffering. God did not send Jesus to the cross as a test of his faith, as punishment for his sin, or to build his character. The Romans crucified Jesus and made him a victim of overt and deadly violence. It was a devastating experience for Jesus' followers who watched him murdered. They were overwhelmed by despair and meaninglessness. They left the scene of the crucifixion feeling abandoned and betrayed by God. The resurrection and subsequent events were the surprising realization that in the midst of profound suffering, God is present and new life is possible. This retrospective realization in no way justified the suffering; it redeemed it. It presented the possibility of new life coming forth from the pain of suffering. Sometimes Jesus' crucifixion is misinterpreted as being the model for suffering. Since Jesus went to the cross, according to the interpretation, persons should bear their own crosses of irrational violence (e.g., rape) without complaint. Rather than the sanctification of suffering, Jesus' crucifixion remains a witness to the horror of violence. It is not a model of how suffering should be born, but a witness to God's desire that no one should have to suffer such violence again. The resurrection, the realization that the Christ was present to the disciples and is present to us, redeemed the suffering and death experience. The people were set free from the pain of that experience to realize the newness of life among them.

In this sense, experiences of suffering, like rape and child sexual abuse, present a victim with an *occasion for new life*, i.e., the occasion to become a survivor. It is an occasion for learning and maturing psychologically and spiritually. Whether or not the experience of suffering indeed becomes this depends largely on the kind of response that the victim receives from family, friends, the Church, and other institutions she/he may encounter. A supportive response will maximize the possibility for healing and new life; a nonsupportive response will to a large degree eliminate such a possibility.

A word of caution is necessary. The awareness that a painful experience like rape or child sexual abuse can be redeemed for the victim is a retrospective insight. Initially, victims do not view their experience in this way. As victims cope with the crisis, reflect on their experience, and integrate their responses, then they may start to experience redemption of the suffering. This process is a long one. Pastors and counselors should not attempt to reassure victims *at this point* that they will certainly grow from their experience of rape! Such a response at the time of the crisis will be heard as uncaring and superficial and as justifying the attack. In the recovery process, and with constructive support, most victims do come to the conclusion that they have grown emotionally and spiritually from the experience. However, the realization should not be put forth prematurely. Also, it should not be suggested as a retrospective explanation of God's activity, for example, "God sent this affliction upon you in order that you might know God's redeeming love and that you might find spiritual growth as a result." God does not send suffering in order to produce this result. God does not will that people should suffer. It is a fact of life that people do suffer. The question is not "why?" but rather "what do people do with that suffering?"

The following illustrates how one victim's awareness of growth reshaped her theology:

> **A young woman was raped at age 18. As a religious person, she reflected on her rape experience in light of her faith. And as she recovered, she observed that her prayer life had shifted dramatically since the assault. Prior to the rape, she recalled that her prayers most often took the form of "Dear God, please take care of me." As she recovered from the rape, she realized that now her prayers began, "Dear God, please help me to remember what I have learned."**

She had moved from a passive, immature relationship with God, in which she expected God to protect her, to a more mature, assertive relationship in which she recognized her own strength and responsibility to care for herself with God's help. In addition, her compassion and empathy for others increased and she was empowered to act to change the things which cause sexual violence. She was able to redeem her experience and mature in her faith as she recovered from the assault with the support and care of her pastor and friends.

Guilt and Shame

Guilt and shame are common reactions for victims of sexual violence. Society has effectively stigmatized victims; they are still regarded as dirty, seen as guilty of sexual indiscretion, and blamed for the attack. Although expression of these attitudes toward victims is often more subtle than before, they still run deep in the individual and collective consciousness of society. Since these attitudes are also held by victims, they have feelings of guilt and shame and do not want anyone to know.[4] For victims who are Christians, there may be additional feelings of guilt and shame stemming from religious teachings.

Much of the guilt and shame about sexual violence which come from religious teachings relate to the confusion of sexuality with sexual violence. If a woman has accepted the Christian teaching that sexual activity outside of marriage is sinful and that women are seductive temptresses, then she will probably view her victimization as a sexual sin and see herself as being responsible. If a male rape victim views his rape as sexual activity rather than violence and if he has learned from Christian teachings that any sexual contact with another male is sinful, then he will probably view his victimization by another man as his own sexual sin. Both victims may feel guilty and shamed by the experience because they see the events as sexual, not violent.

This feeling of shame is particularly poignant for victims who are sexually inexperienced. Seeing their rape experience as sexual, they feel that they have "lost their virginity." This is most difficult for women in a culture where there still remains a vestige of patriarchal attitudes which regard women as property and regard unmarried women who are not virgins as "damaged goods." Victims in this circumstance are dealing not only with the crisis of sexual assault, but also with their fear that their entire future is jeopardized.

In situations where the Christian victim of sexual violence feels guilt and shame, pastors or counselors, by acknowledging the guilt and shame which may be present, can help the victim to look for the source of these feelings, i.e., societal and/or religious teachings which are erroneous. Since the chances are good that a victim will be confusing the experience of sexual violence with sexual activity, this distinction needs to be clarified and discussed. This is most important for sexually inexperienced victims so that they do not assume that all sexual activity is coercive or violent.

Clarification and discussion distinguishing sexual from violent is also needed when the victim's primary concern is "loss of virginity." While *technically* rape may destroy the symbol of virginity (i.e., for a woman, it may rupture the hymen), this experience is no more related to a person's first *sexual* experience than is a woman's first gynecological examination (which also may rupture the hymen). In addition to this clarification, however, some women will need to come to terms with the high priority they may have placed on their virginity, which, unfortunately, is often reinforced by religious teachings (e.g., the teaching derived from St. Maria Goretti discussed earlier). For some women this priority means that their identity is based on their value as a sexual commodity.[5]

In fact, a woman who sees her own value as primarily a function of whether or not she can present herself to a husband as a technical virgin (i.e., hymen intact) has a very limited and distorted sense of self-worth. In her recovery process, she will need to develop a more integrated sense of self-worth. She is worthy because she is a person created in God's image. Her worth derives from her personhood, not her value as a sexual commodity.[6]

Abandonment by God

Some victims talk about feeling left alone in the midst of suffering as being abandoned by God. There are two possible sources for their feelings of abandonment. One is the lack of support and involvement by family and friends. When people avoid the victim, she/he may literally experience being abandoned by those closest to her/him. She/he may then assume that God has also turned away. A second source of the feeling of abandonment comes from the victim's experience and understanding of suffering. As was discussed previously, if a person believes God to be omnipotent, loving, and rewarding of the righteousness of good Christians, then suffering is either a sign of God's disfavor or a realization that God does not play by the rules. Either interpretation can lead to the feeling of being abandoned by God. This feeling of abandonment occurs for the victim who expected God to protect her from all pain and suffering. When she encounters suffering, she feels betrayed. The sense of abandonment by God is profound and often creates a crisis of faith for the victim.

Victims' sense of abandonment is expressed in various ways. It may be articulated as having difficulty with prayer: "I pray, but God doesn't seem to hear me . . ." or "I can't ever pray anymore." Or the experience may center on a realization that a male God and a male redeemer cannot comprehend a woman's experience of victimization. God's "maleness," reasons the victim, makes God worthless to her in her suffering. She feels abandoned by a God who cannot understand. She may simply feel numb and out of touch with God: "I don't know where God is in all of this." Subsequently, a victim may feel guilt: "I seem to have lost all of my faith—it must not have been very strong to begin with." She may feel anger mixed with despair: "Where is God now when I am hurting and need help?"

A pastor or counselor can reassure a victim that these feelings are normal under the circumstances and a common experience for victims. They even appear in Scripture, for example,

> *My God, my God, why has thou forsaken me?*
> *Why art thou so far from helping me, from the*
>   *words of my groaning?*
> *O my God, I cry by day, but thou dost not answer;*
>   *and by night, but find no rest. . . .*
> *Be not far from me, for trouble is near*
>   *and there is none to help.*
>
> *Psalm 22:1–2, 11*[7]

These words of Scripture are echoed in Jesus' despair as he cried from the cross: "My God, my God, why hast thou forsaken me?" Here even Jesus' faith faltered; in the midst of the physical and emotional pain of crucifixion and impending death, he too felt abandoned by God: "Why have you left me here alone? Why have you given me up to this terrifying experience?" The fear that we will be left totally alone to face suffering and even death reaches to the depths of our being and confronts our faith.

If a person believes that the sign of God's presence is protection from suffering, the experience of suffering logically indicates God's absence. This expectation is based on an understanding of God as one who omnipotently intervenes in human affairs protecting some but not others. While this view of God is often the basis of Biblical prayers and requests, it is not the predominant image of God that is experienced by the people. God does not promise to protect us from all suffering as long as we behave properly and follow the rules. God knows that we will all suffer. What God does promise is to be present with us even in that suffering—to strengthen and carry us through. God did not reach out and snatch Jesus off

the cross in order to protect him from the pain. But God was
faithful to Jesus through that experience.

> As I sat with a group of mothers of incest victims (women
> whose husbands or ex-husbands had sexually abused their
> children), the theme of feeling abandoned by God came up
> several times. Finally, one woman told of her experience:
> She said that before she was aware of the incest and had to
> face this crisis in her family, she had pictured her relation-
> ship with God as two sets of footprints on the beach. God
> always walked beside her in her life and she knew that God
> was always there with her. After the incest crisis began, her
> picture of her relationship with God shifted. Now she only
> saw one set of footprints on the beach. In her despair, she
> assumed that God no longer walked with her. Only later, as
> the crisis began to be resolved, did she look again at the
> image and make a different interpretation. In retrospect, she
> saw that the single set of footprints on the beach were God's
> footprints. Her's were missing because God was carrying her
> through the crisis.

A victim who feels that God has abandoned her/him cannot
be convinced of God's faithfulness and presence by even the
most persuasive and articulate pastor or counselor. The victim
will only know it through her/his own experience. We can
accept and not condemn this feeling of abandonment, mindful
of the fact that even Jesus experienced the same feeling. We
can identify with her/his fear and bear witness to our own
experience of God's presence in our lives in times of suffering.
Furthermore, our presence can mediate God's presence during a victim's recovery from an assault.

Anger

Virtually every victim of sexual violence experiences anger at
some point, either during or after the assault or abuse. This

anger is a healthy response to victimization. Yet for Christians, it is often an uncomfortable feeling which may be repressed. Christians in general and Christian women in particular have learned from various sources that all anger is sinful and unbecoming to a woman. Thus, victims not only may repress their anger, but may also feel guilty about experiencing it at all. Some victims are so well socialized not to express anger that their anger may not surface until years after the abuse. This is particularly common for victims of child sexual abuse who discover their anger as adults when they begin to deal with their childhood abuse.

In providing pastoral care for victims, we need to assist them in uncovering their anger and directing it appropriately. For those who are already expressing anger, we can affirm and assist them in focusing it. Affirmation and support for feelings of anger can begin with a clarification of righteous anger. Righteous anger is anger for a right reason and an appropriate response to a situation of injustice. Jesus' response to the money lenders in the temple was righteous anger (John 2:14–22). Anger is an appropriate and valid response to the abuse of a person. We can give permission to victims to be angry and to feel no guilt. Revenge, however, is not the same as righteous anger and should be challenged by a pastor or counselor. Not only does revenge cut short any process of justice, it also can easily become self-destructive for the victim. For example, if a victim goes after her rapist a week after the rape and kills him, she will be charged with murder. The victim's act of revenge could result in her imprisonment. Justice is not served by such an act.

Anger in response to sexual violence may initially be undirected or misdirected. The rage may be so powerful that it immobilizes the victim. The victim may need help in focusing and directing her anger.

A young woman who had been raped expressed strong feelings of anger at God for having "let" the rape happen to her. The power of her anger and the fact that she directed it

toward God frightened her. I suggested that she write a letter to God expressing her anger. I reminded her that God could handle her angry feelings and she did not need to hold back to protect God. She wrote the letter and decided to share it with me the next time we talked. It went on for three pages lambasting God for allowing there to be such a thing as rape and for not protecting her from it.

After this letter-writing exercise, which expurgated the woman of much of her rage, we were able to discuss her understanding of God and of suffering sufficiently to enable her to move beyond "blaming God." Her anger was affirmed: The world did not end because she lashed out at God. It was then redirected toward the real source of her suffering.

Sometimes the anger is directed toward the victim's partner or at a family member. Sometimes pastors or counselors find the rage pouring forth at them. It is important for the persons on the receiving end of the anger to understand that they may be getting it simply because they are there at that moment. It may have nothing to do with them personally. It can make them feel very uncomfortable or even attacked, which may call forth their defenses. They may be tempted to respond, "Why are you yelling at me? I didn't rape you!" A more helpful approach is to be aware of the limit on being the depository for this initial anger. Once the limit is reached, the pastor or counselor should encourage the victim to focus the anger on the source of her/his suffering and to express it appropriately. The anger is affirmed but not allowed to harm others.

When the victim's anger is directed inward, the result can be self-destructive. For example, an adult, who had been a childhood victim of incestuous abuse and who had not been able to deal with this experience, found herself in a pattern of heavy drug abuse. Another victim who, as a teenager, suffered chronic sexual abuse by a neighbor and received no support from her family, made repeated suicide attempts.

Both of these victims turned their anger toward themselves. To enable victims to break their self-destructive patterns and to begin the healing process, they should be assisted in the following:

- the identification of the source(s) of their abuse;
- the placement of the responsibility for the abuse with those sources;
- the direction of the victim's anger at those sources.

Directing the anger at the source of the suffering is vital if a victim is to be able to move through the process of recovery and healing. There may be multiple sources: initially, the offender, and, secondarily, the system which may have been nonsupportive or even further victimized the victim. The insensitive police officer or medical doctor who reacted with disbelief to the victim's story; the unscrupulous defense attorney who tried to smear the victim's reputation as a defense for his/her client; the minister who encouraged the victim to pray and forget about the assault; the rape crisis counselor who ignored a victim's need to deal with her/his religious concerns—all of these represent the system's responses which could compound the victimization. The victim may need assistance in identifying the sources and in focusing her/his anger.

A victim's anger as a healthy and appropriate response to victimization motivates the victim to act on her/his own behalf. When it is directed outward towards the appropriate source, it energizes the victim.

A victim was hesitant to report her assault to the police because she was anxious about the long, involved legal process which would result. As she got in touch with her anger not only at what the rapist had done to her, but also at what he would continue to do to other women, she decided to report the rape. She went through with the prosecution of her assailant.

Her anger enabled her to act and to do what she could to insure that the rapist would not rape again.

While righteous anger is a healthy response to victimization, it represents a stage in the healing process, not a way of life. Sometimes the victim's anger becomes the center of her life. This all-consuming anger can drain all of her energy and make it difficult for her to take care of herself or act in her own behalf. While people cannot be talked out of their anger, they can be encouraged to utilize it and move through it, not holding on to it longer than necessary.

Forgiveness

For the Christian victim, being able to let go of the anger and move on is related to being able to forgive. The question of forgiveness is often raised initially by someone other than the victim. A friend or family member may urge: "Forgive and forget—there's nothing you can do about it now." A pastor or counselor may question: "Isn't it time you forgave him? If God can forgive him, surely you can, too." For a victim who does not *feel* forgiving at this point, these words of advice only leave her/him feeling guilty for not forgiving and estranged from those attempting to assist her/him.

An act of forgiveness by a victim cannot be hurried; nor can it be orchestrated by those on the outside. To expect people to move quickly from their pain to forgive those who are responsible for it is insensitive and unrealistic. Forgiveness is not merely an act of will, although it is an intentional, willful act. One cannot just decide "I will forgive" because someone else suggests one *should* forgive.

Forgiveness is a word which has become more and more meaningless in our society. Some people mean that they want to simply forget what happened—just put it out of their mind. Others mean by forgiving that the offense or injury which occurred is okay, i.e., that somehow it becomes a non-offense. Neither of these meanings is adequate to the experience of rape or sexual abuse. A person can never forget these offenses. The memory of the event will always be in the victim's consciousness. It becomes a part of one's history as do one's positive experiences. And nothing can ever make the offense a non-offense. It will never be okay that a person was raped or molested. It is forever a wrong done to another human being.

For Christians, forgiving is one means of letting go and disarming the power that the offense has over a victim's life.

> I will no longer allow this experience to dominate my life. I will not let it continue to make me feel bad about myself. I will not let it limit my ability to love and trust others in my life. I will not let my memory of the experience continue to victimize and control me.

Forgiving means letting go of the anger and putting the rape experience in perspective: "I can never forget what happened. But I choose to put it here and leave it behind. If I ever need to recall it, I know where it is. But I refuse to carry the pain any longer." Forgiving means acknowledging the humanness of the offender: "I refuse to let his acts toward me prevent me from recognizing his humanity, that, like me, he is created in God's image." But forgiving never means condoning or excusing what he did: "What he did is a distortion of who he was created to be and should never have happened." Forgiving does not mean allowing oneself to be abused repeatedly: "Take heed to yourselves; if your brother sins, *rebuke him* [emphasis added], and *if he repents* [emphasis added], forgive him; and if he sins against you seven times in the day, and turns to you seven times, and says, 'I repent,' you must forgive him." (Luke 17: 3–4). Jesus teaches that a person must be willing to confront the offense and be willing to forgive as many times as it takes. But it is also clear in this Scripture that a person's forgiveness is dependent on the offender's repentance.

Forgiveness does not just happen nor is it unconditional. In human experience[8] forgiveness occurs within a context and takes place when a set of conditions are met. In order to be authentic, forgiveness must be based on the following:

- a conscious choice on the part of the victim to let go of that experience of pain and anger;
- empowerment of the victim through God's grace;
- an experience of justice by the victim.

The choice on the part of the victim to let go only happens *when she/he is ready to let go*. When the healing is sufficient and the victim feels strong enough, she/he will be ready to forgive and can make that choice. Even then, it is not easy to let go. God's grace, which is known through prayer and the presence of the Holy Spirit, can enpower a victim to forgive. Finally, in order to forgive, the victim needs some experience of justice. At some point in the aftermath of a rape or the disclosure of sexual abuse, a victim needs some concrete expression of the fact that she/he has been wronged, that what occurred should never have happened, and that the offender is responsible. Ideally, the offender's repentance will provide that justice and will free the victim to forgive. As the Gospel says, "if he repents, forgive him." (See the following section, "Confession and Repentance.") But the offender's repentance cannot be guaranteed. On occasion, the legal system can provide an expression of justice, for example, when the rapist is apprehended and convicted. In other situations, victims experience no sense of justice from the legal system, e.g., when a rapist is convicted of the assault but then his conviction is overturned on appeal because of a legal technicality and he is released into the community. The experience of justice may come from sources other than the legal system. It may be very simple. For example, a teenager finally reveals to a teacher whom she trusts that her father has been sexually abusing her for six years. The teacher believes her and acts to protect her from further abuse. One person standing up for her/him may be sufficient for the victim to experience justice. Whatever form it takes, justice is a prerequisite for a victim to move towards forgiveness.

Most importantly, forgiveness happens in its own time and cannot be rushed from the outside. It may take one year or thirty. Pastors or counselors can be available to a victim as she/he struggles with a need and desire to forgive. They can do whatever they can to mediate justice in her/his experience. They can bear witness to God's presence and power. But they cannot force a victim to forgive.

Confession and Repentance

One of the major religious issues in working with offenders as opposed to victims is the issue of confession and repentance. The willingness on the part of rapists or child molesters to admit what they have done and to acknowledge the harm that their actions have caused another person are significant steps for sex offenders. In religious terms, these constitute confession. A sex offender may seek out a pastor for the purpose of confessing. Too often, however, an offender will confess to a pastor, ask for forgiveness and, having received cheap grace, walk away believing everything is fine. His confession may be honest, his remorse real, and his desire for forgiveness authentic, but he also wants it to be easy. A word from the pastor, a quick prayer, and all is well; he then believes he will stop sexually abusing his daughter. Seldom, if ever, is this sufficient to stop a sex offender, because his confession has fallen short of repentance. Confession is necessary, but not sufficient. It is only a first step toward repentance. Dietrich Bonhoeffer comments: ". . . A man who confesses his sins in the presence of a brother knows he is no longer alone with himself; he experiences the presence of God in the reality of the other person."[9] Thus, confession can reconnect an offender with God's presence which can then empower him to repent.

Repentance goes beyond confession, apology, and good intentions. Repentance means to turn around, to change one's behavior, and to not repeat the offense.[10] If one does not do whatever is necessary to change one's abusive behavior, then confession is at best a sham and at worst a ploy.[11] What is necessary for the sex offender in most cases is a long and difficult process of treatment (which may or may not involve incarceration). In a treatment situation, the offender's faith can provide the source of strength and determination he needs to stay in treatment. In addition, the supportive but firm position of the pastor ("I want you to be in that treatment group every week; this is God's will for you now.") can encourage the offender's commitment to the treatment process.

For the pastor or counselor, caution is advised especially in the situation where an offender "gets religion" soon after his offense is disclosed: "Now that I've found Jesus Christ, I am a new person—I'll never rape again. I don't need to see a counselor now that I have Jesus in my heart." His sudden conversion may be a ploy to avoid treatment. Or his religious experience may be genuine, in which case he sincerely believes he will not offend again. In either case, a pastor or counselor must avoid being taken in by the offender's good intentions. Realizing that the offender will offend again unless he gets help, the pastor or counselor must insist that he seek the treatment he needs. All things are possible through God, even the rehabilitation of a sex offender. His repentance becomes real as he makes the effort to change. Jeremiah's vision of the potter is a reminder: "So I went down to the potter's house, and there he was working at his wheel. And the vessel he was making of clay was spoiled in the potter's hand, and he reworked it into another vessel, as it seemed good to the potter to do" (Jeremiah 18:3-4). Change is possible.

Reconciliation—When Repentance Meets Forgiveness

Reconciliation means to bring together that which should be together in right relationship, to renew a broken relationship on new terms, and to heal the injury of broken trust which has resulted from an offense inflicted by one person on another. If justice is the right relation between persons, than reconciliation is the making of justice where there was injustice. Reconciliation happens when the offender repents and the injured forgives, creating the possibility of a new relationship. Unfortunately, this ideal of reconciliation seldom is manifest, especially in cases of sexual violence. The victim's hurt may be too deep for her/him to be able to forgive; or the offender's denial and unwillingness to take responsibility may be too strong for him/her to be able to repent. The offender may be dead and gone as is sometimes the case when incestuous abuse is finally acknowledged; or the victim may have no interest in reconciling a relationship with a stranger who assaulted her. Nevertheless, reconciliation remains a worthwhile goal in situations where there has been sexual violence.

One act which can enhance the possibility of reconciliation between victim and offender is restitution on the part of the offender. When restitution follows from repentance, it is a concrete act which assures the victim of the offender's honest intentions and desire to right the relationship. Restitution may take the form of payment to the victim for medical expenses or payment to a rape crisis center to support their services. Sometimes restitution is ordered by the court, sometimes it is voluntary. Restitution can be one step that leads toward reconciliation. For example:

> **A woman who had not seen her father since she had left home seven years earlier decided to write to him and confront him with the sexual abuse he had inflicted on her in her childhood and teenage years. He wrote her back and asked to visit her.**

She agreed, somewhat reluctantly. When they met, he acknowledged the abuse and told her that he now realized that what he had done was wrong. She let him know how angry she was and that she was still dealing with the psychological aftereffects in therapy and with physical discomfort from urinary infections that resulted from the abuse. His remorse and sense of responsibility were real. He offered to pay for her medical and counseling expenses. He said he had talked with his pastor who had encouraged him to meet with her. He asked her to forgive him. She felt herself tighten, afraid once again of betrayal. And then she felt herself begin to let go of the anger. It had served its purpose; it had motivated her to confront her father. She questioned him about other children; had he abused them, too? She found that she had been the only one, an only child, and that he had not gone out of the family. But he realized his problem was still there and his pastor had urged him to see a counselor. He had already had two sessions. Her anger dissipated further. For the first time, she saw him beginning to take responsibility for himself. She said she forgave him mostly so that she could get on with her life. She said she hoped that he would stay in therapy and work on his problems because she couldn't help him. They agreed to visit each other again when both felt up to it. She agreed to let him see her children, his grandchildren, whom he had never met, but only under a clear understanding that he would not take advantage of them. She explained that she had taught them to tell her if *any* adult tried to touch them sexually. He assured her he would not hurt them. He visited her family for holidays and was able to have a satisfying relationship with his daughter's family thereafter, never forgetting but never discussing again the sexual abuse from years earlier.

Although the ideal is difficult and seldom attained, it is worth looking toward as a possibility. In so doing, we must realize that forgiveness or repentance alone cannot accomplish reconciliation. But when both meet, the possibility is real. No longer, then, is the victim or the offender defined by the offense, but once again they are two persons whose brokenness is healed and who can encounter each other anew.

Honor Your Father and Mother

The Sunday school teaching of the Commandment to honor father and mother presents special difficulty for the child who is being sexually abused by her/his parent(s) and for the parents. If the parent misuses this teaching to demand unquestioning obedience from a child, then the incest victim is compelled to submit to sexual activity with the parent and to feel guilty if she/he questions such activity. The victim feels that there is no recourse because not only is parental authority invoked, but also religious authority: This is the teaching of the Bible and the Church.

This misuse of scriptural teaching is a blatant distortion. In Ephesians, Paul makes very clear the meaning of the Commandment:

> Children, obey your parents *in the Lord* [emphasis added], for this is right. "Honor your father and mother" (this is the first commandment with a promise) "that it may be well with you and that you may live long on the earth." Fathers, do not provoke your children to anger, but bring them up *in the discipline and instruction of the Lord* [emphasis added].
>
> Ephesians 6:1–4

Children's obedience to parents is conditional; it is to be "in the Lord," i.e., consistent with the Gospel. Here, in addition to the reminder to children to keep this Commandment, there are instructions to parents: Guide and instruct your children in Christian values such as love, mercy, compassion, and justice. The caution to the father not to provoke the child to anger is most telling and appropriate. Nothing provokes a child's anger more quickly than abuse by a parent, especially sexual abuse.

A child victim of incestuous abuse (or an adult who was a child victim) may need help in resolving questions about this religious teaching on relationships with parents before she/he can address any other religious concerns. Incestuous abuse clearly violates the parent's responsibility and in no way deserves to be excused or allowed based on this Commandment.

Notes

1. Harold Kushner, *When Bad Things Happen To Good People* (New York: Schocken Books, 1981), p. 88.
2. But the explanation does not adequately explain the cause of suffering unrelated to human activity, e.g., earthquake, volcano, or hurricane. Harold Kushner's book titled *When Bad Things Happen to Good People* is an excellent resource in discussion of the topic of suffering.
3. This question reflected a common belief in Hebrew theology at that time. Raymond E. Brown, S.S., Joseph A. Fitzmyer, S.J., Roland E. Murphy, O. Carm., *The Jerome Biblical Commentary* (Englewood Cliffs, N.J.: Prentice-Hall, 1969), p. 443 and C. K. Barrett, *Gospel According to St. John* (London: S.P.C.K., 1955), p. 294.
4. The desire to conceal a sexual attack is particularly strong among teenagers, who may fear the reaction of their peers and risk ostracization from the group.
5. "The 'goodness' of women was defined in terms of their desirability as objects of an exclusive sexual relationship; a 'good' woman, therefore, was a woman who resisted all temptation to squander her limited resources and who fought to preserve her assets for the man who could rightfully lay claim to them. . . . Since women's sexual and reproductive capacities were the qualities which men bargained and paid for, female sexuality became a commodity, and like any other commodity it had various price tags. It was thus inevitable that valuable female sexual property would on occasion be stolen. . . ." Lorenne Clark and Debra Lewis, *Rape: The Price of Coercive Sexuality*

(Toronto: Women's Educational Press, 1977), pp. 172–73.

6. This specific concern about loss of virginity may be a priority for particular ethnic or religious groups, e.g., Latina or Muslim women, and should be dealt with sensitively, respecting the individual's religious and cultural heritage.

7. The Psalms are filled with supplications to God, requests for protection, and also testimony of God's presence and support. Clearly the fear that God would abandon them was common in the people's experience, an experience often of violence and oppression.

8. Some argue that we should follow Christ's model of forgiveness from the Cross in which he unconditionally forgave those who crucified him. This was an act of forgiveness of which Jesus was capable because he was the Christ. As human beings, we do not share that capability when faced with our own experiences of suffering. However, Jesus' teaching in the Gospels helps provide the context from which we can forgive our offenders.

9. Dietrich Bonhoeffer, *Life Together*, trans. John W. Doberstein (New York: Harper & Row, 1954), p. 116, as cited in Doris Donnelly, *Learning to Forgive* (New York: Macmillan, 1979), p. 68.

10. "For the Jew the Hebrew term 'teshuvah' is the word for repentance. 'Teshuvah' literally means 'return,' clearly denoting a return to God after sin. In Judaism there is a distinction between sins against God and sins against people. For the former only regret or confession is necessary. For sins against people, 'teshuvah' requires three steps: first, admission of wrongdoing; second, asking for forgiveness of the person wronged (here abused); third, reconciliation which can be accomplished only by a change in behavior." Marie M. Fortune and Judith Hertz in *Family Violence: A Workshop Manual for Clergy and Other Service Providers* (Seattle, Wa.: The Center for the Prevention of Sexual and Domestic Violence, 1980), p. 78.

11. This notion is not intended to present a debate between justification by faith versus justification by works. It is rather to suggest that repentance is not only in word but in deed as well.

Chapter 11

COMMUNITY OF FAITH

The Church as a community of faith carries a pastoral responsibility to victims and offenders of sexual violence. The community of faith as we have experienced it in the Christian tradition is made up of believers, those who confess faith in God and who seek to live their lives accordingly based on the Gospels. It is no surprise that the community of faith is a diverse grouping ranging from those with fundamentalist theologies to those with liberation theologies. The community of faith gathers in a structured format (congregation or parish) or a nonstructured one (house church, liberation church, shalom meal). Wherever and however the community of faith gathers, it claims to be a part of the body of Christ and, through it, we are called to ministry.

Congregational Response

In the context of sexual violence, how is this ministry manifest in the life of a congregation? How can a congregation individually and collectively respond to victims of sexual violence and their families? It is important to recognize that congregations (and individuals) react to the suffering of a rape victim with deep ambivalence.

Congregations seem to respond to people's pain based on an unspoken standard of differential suffering. If a member shares with the pastor and congregation the news that her father died yesterday, the congregation would respond with cards, prayers, flowers, visits, assistance with the funeral, family meals, and hosting out-of-town guests. If that same member shares that she was raped yesterday by her employer, the congregation would most likely not know what to do and might well do nothing.

For some kinds of suffering, congregations and pastors are comfortable in the Good Samaritan role. For other kinds— like the personal, bodily suffering of sexual violence— congregations too often play the Priest and the Levite and pass by on the other side. It is no surprise that victims seldom seek the support of their congregations, anticipating the ambivalence and discomfort they will most likely encounter.

Congregational ambivalence is but a reflection of our own individual ambivalence. Most people, even those who are more aware, have a lingering question as to whether a rape victim is not somehow responsible for her/his assault. Like Job's comforters, we may try to be helpful, but we may also be trying to discern what the victim must have done to deserve this suffering (see Chapter 10, "Religious Concerns and Pastoral Issues").

Part of our motivation for focusing on how she/he may have deserved this suffering is to reassure ourselves that it will not happen to us. We simply will never let ourselves be in a position to "deserve" this suffering. In addition, we have a need to dissociate ourselves from a victim, particularly a victim who is similar to us (in age, race, class, lifestyle, etc.). If we allow ourselves to acknowledge that this victim is very much like us and that she/he was assaulted, then we have to face the reality that we may also become a victim. To keep this realization at a distance, we keep the victim at a distance. Being with the victim is a too painful reminder of our own vulnerability. So the person who was victimized is isolated and denied the support of her community of faith.

An alternative congregational response to a victim of sexual violence would focus on presence. Rather than shying away, we can be present, available, and willing to listen. Some victims prefer to tell their story to others; other victims prefer not to repeat it. In either case, we should not avoid the issue by talking about the weather; the pretense of normality leads victims to believe we do not want to talk about the assault at all. We can reassure the victim that we still care about her/him. We should be honest about our feelings by being willing to say that what has happened to her/him makes us uncomfortable or frightened. Our pretense to be unaffected by her/his experience sets us apart from her/him. We can also be present by offering to help, e.g., by taking a woman's children on a day's outing or preparing dinner for her family one evening. In these ways, the members of the victim's community of faith can be present, supportive, and caring, and thereby help the victim to avoid isolation from a significant source of support.

The congregational response to a sex offender is equally ambivalent and difficult. Often there seem to be three choices: a congregation will support an offender's denial that he is responsible for the offense; or, believing his guilt, ostracize him completely from the congregation; or ignore the whole issue altogether. All of these responses communicate that we as a congregation cannot deal with someone among us who is a sex offender. So we deny the evidence that he is an offender ("How could he be? He teaches Sunday school and sings in the choir"), and support his denial even to providing character witnesses at his trial. If we accept the evidence, we make it clear that the offender is unwelcome in the community of faith. Or we pretend to be unaware of the situation entirely. None of these responses is helpful to the offender nor to any efforts to make justice and reconciliation possible.

The community of faith, particularly in the form of the congregation, seems to find it virtually impossible to confront a sex offender by indicating unequivocally that his behavior, which is harmful to others, is wrong and must stop, and by refusing to excuse, explain away, or minimize what he has done. Simultaneously, we seem unable to be supportive and affirming of the offender's efforts to change, to make restitution, and to seek reconciliation. In short, we have difficulty speaking the truth in love and holding each other accountable for something as serious as sexual violence.

A person who rapes or sexually abuses others is not aided by our denial of the evidence of this fact, just as an alcoholic is not helped when we overlook his/her periodic intoxication. Likewise, our minimization of the offense serves no useful purpose. Comments like "these things just happen sometimes," or "could have happened to anybody," or "boys will be boys," give the offender the impression that what happened was not really serious. In the face of these responses, the offender feels no motivation to change. We must be willing to communicate clearly and directly our disapproval of his offending behavior; we must be willing to speak the truth.

A sex offender who is confronted with his offense by the victim, the legal system, his congregation, friends, or family is not helped by being ostracized. This only furthers his isolation and hostility, which makes it difficult for him to try to change. He is not helped by being the focus of vengeful attacks, verbal or physical. A group of people who are willing to be supportive, to strengthen his resolve to stay in a treatment program, to be present with him through the process of change is what is most needed. Ostracism is punishment which does not bring change. To be present in love to the offender is to bring a supportive and firm hand to bear in order to enable his repentance and possible reconciliation.

Liturgical Supports

One of the unique aspects of the community of faith as it seeks to respond to victims of sexual violence is its potential for supporting a victim's recovery through a liturgical form. Just as we give form to other significant experiences through baptism, weddings, and funerals, it is also appropriate that we seek liturgical ways to bring healing and resolution to victims. Most of the liturgical activities which have arisen in response to victims have taken place informally, outside of a congregational setting. The following three examples illustrate the ways liturgy has been used to further a victim's healing process.

> A woman who had been raped realized that she felt somehow stained by the assault. It was not that she felt dirty or stigmatized by the sexual contact *per se*. Rather, in the violation of her person, she felt that something had been put on her which she could not cast off. So she decided that she wanted to experience some form of ritual cleansing in order to be cleansed of the violation. She sought the help of a woman minister friend who suggested that she gather her close friends and then use water to wash away the stain of violation.

Having her friends present, her community of faith which affirmed her worth as a person, provided a reminder that she was not alone in her experience. The ritual restored her sense of wholeness and well-being physically, emotionally, and spiritually. She felt renewed and no longer defined by the rape experience.

> A woman was raped in her own apartment. As the first anniversary of her rape approached, she began to feel anxious. She was fearful of making it through the night which would be one year since her rape. Since she is Roman Catholic, she decided to utilize a traditional liturgical form to assist her. She arranged to hold a vigil throughout the night of this anniversary. She held vigil alone in her apartment. She knew that her friends were also awake in their homes praying with her through the night. The next morning she and her friends gathered with a priest to celebrate mass.

This vigil experience enabled her to redeem that date, to regain control over that night which a year ago had been so devastating to her. By staying awake and sharing prayer with her community of faith, she knew that the night itself would no longer hold power over her.

A seminary intern was raped by a stranger early one afternoon as she was working alone in the church where she was employed for the summer. A man cornered her in the church office and sexually assaulted her. The safety which she had felt here in this quiet suburban congregation was shattered by the attack. Like any other rape victim, she began the long and painful process of recovery which was made all the more difficult by her having to arrive each day for work at the church where her assault took place. At the end of the summer, the woman left the community to return to seminary, unsure about the future of her vocation as a woman in ministry. In some ways, the rape had become a symbol of her relationship with the church—a relationship which was painful, angering, sobering, and yet which still held potential for new life.

The next year at seminary and a lot of counsel and support from friends and colleagues brought clarity to her vocational commitment and she responded to a call to the ordained ministry. She chose to be ordained in the church where she was raped. She chose to return to that place where not only had she known the ultimate vulnerability, but also the joy of fellowship and the promise of celebration. She chose to lay claim to that place which had claimed her several years before.

Her ordination became a significant moment of transition for her. She moved from being a victim to being a survivor, from being a victim to being a minister. In that event, she was made new—the place was made new. Her ordination redeemed that physical space for her. Once again, it became a place of joy and celebration, a source of new life which empowered her rather than rendering her powerless.

This woman could very easily not have returned to seminary to complete her training and enter the ministry. She could have quietly withdrawn and privately nursed her wound. But because of her courage and her willingness to receive the support of her community of faith, she remained open to her call. She refused to allow a rapist to hold her back from the ministry she knew she must do. Because of her experience as a victim, her response to victims of all kinds has special integrity; her compassion for their suffering and her anger at the sources of their suffering carry her forward uniquely prepared to minister with the people.

The community of faith can be a valuable resource to victims and offenders. This is possible only as its members are able and willing to open their eyes to the reality of sexual violence. A congregation's fear and discomfort can be reduced as information is presented and discussed. By being more informed, a community of faith is prepared to respond to the pain of a member dealing with sexual violence. An individual's community of faith can provide the pastoral and liturgical support she/he needs.

Chapter 12

STRATEGIES FOR ACTION

Responding to sexual violence is like responding to the problem of cancer. Effective strategies are implemented in multiple ways: there are after-the-fact and before-the-fact strategies, individual and collective actions. Millions of dollars are spent each year to find a "cure" for cancer. This is basically an after-the-fact approach. The dollars are used to answer the question of how to cure a cancer that has already taken hold in the body. Solutions to this problem are certainly necessary, but they are only Band-Aids; they are necessary but insufficient to eliminate cancer. Before-the-fact strategies include health precautions: avoiding too much sun, not smoking, etc. These precautions are helpful but are limited to those things over which we as individuals have control. The larger sources of cancer must also be addressed, e.g., workers must be protected from occupational hazards like asbestos poisoning. Finally the sources of carcinogens must be eliminated, e.g., the water supply contaminated by chemical dumping, leaks from nuclear reactors, etc. Our efforts in response to sexual violence are similar.

Pastoral response to victims and offenders, rape crisis services, etc. are after-the-fact responses. While a vital necessity for the well-being of rape victims, they do very little to prevent rape. Our efforts to respond to sexual violence must also be before-the-fact. When people begin to ask what can be done before-the-fact about sexual violence, their questions are usually very personalized and individual. For example, "How can I keep from being raped? How can I protect my children from a child molester?" Their proposed solutions are equally individualized: "I never go out after dark anymore. I do not allow my children to walk to school anymore." The problem with most people's strategies in response to sexual violence is that they focus on avoiding personal attack, are often based on misinformation about sexual assault, and do not utilize collective resources for action. In addition, these individualized efforts to avoid attack often result in limiting people's activities. Such limitations serve in turn to increase people's passivity and fear. For example, the churchwoman who no longer goes to evening meetings because she is afraid to go out at night may avoid an attack but she becomes more isolated and passive. This is a high price to pay for a sense of safety. Furthermore, this woman is still at risk even though she stays home. She is almost as likely to be attacked in her own home as she is on the street. Her sense of safety is somewhat illusory. An individual's limitations on her/his activities may protect that person from a sexual assault, but these actions do very little to prevent sexual assault in general from occurring.

An effective before-the-fact strategy to end sexual violence must include activity in three areas: precautions, protection, and prevention. Precautions are steps taken to minimize or avoid potential dangers; protection includes steps taken when someone is faced with immediate danger; and prevention describes activity to address the danger at its roots and to eliminate it. Precautions, protection, and prevention are strategies that are implemented by persons working both individually and collectively.

Precautions are steps taken by individuals or groups to minimize potential dangers. These would include keeping doors locked, avoiding hitchhiking, maintaining adequate street lighting, organizing a block watch, etc. Precautions are intended to help a person avoid contact with a potential attacker. It is critical that precautions be based on accurate information about sexual assault. For example, people who decide that they will never open their door to a stranger are only addressing forty percent of the dangerous situations: Sixty percent of rapists are known to their victims, i.e., a friend, acquaintance, family member, co-worker. Another example is that people who resolve never to go out of their home alone in order to avoid rapists are only safe half the time: Fifty percent of all rapes occur in someone's home. Or the child who is taught to stay away from strangers or not to take rides from strangers is only prepared for fifteen percent of assaultive situations: Eighty-five percent of all sexual abuse against children is inflicted by someone known to them and usually someone well-known. Precautions are helpful only if they are based on the reality of sexual assault situations.

Protection refers to the steps a person takes when confronted by an attacker. Protecting one's self means defending oneself physically or verbally. In order to be effective, self-defense also has to be based on an accurate understanding of sexual assault. For example, if a person is approached at a bus stop by a suspicious-looking person who attempts to begin a conversation, ignoring him may not be as effective as assertively and verbally turning down such conversation. Being able to defend oneself adequately requires training and practice. For example, persons who carry guns or mace cans without having specific training may increase their danger. The weapons of unprepared victims are often used against them. Self-defense programs are a means of protection. Through specialized programs, children, teenagers, and adults can learn physical and verbal skills, gain self-confidence, and overcome fears about being able to defend themselves.[1]

For some Christian women, the whole idea of preparing to protect oneself from the violence of sexual assault is difficult to consider. Our religious training may make it hard for us to consider seriously the possibility that we too may be victims; and even if we do accept that possibility, our religious training may prevent us from adequately preparing to protect ourselves. There are several aspects of religious teaching (primarily directed at girls and women) that get in the way of consideration of our own self-protection.

- A belief that "good" women do not get raped; only "bad" women get raped—Proper, virtuous behavior or religious piety do not guarantee one's safety. God does not "protect" the righteous and allow the unrighteous to be harmed. Rape is not something that girls and women bring on by the way they dress or behave or by where they go. Every female in our society is at risk for some form of sexual attack. Being a "good, Christian woman" does not lessen vulnerability.
- A confusion between propriety and appropriateness— As women we have been taught to be kind and polite to others; as Christians, we have been taught kindness and concern, not to speak harshly to others, etc. Under ordinary circumstances, these are reasonable and admirable ways to interact with someone else. But when we are confronted by a rapist, gentle, kind words are seldom effective; this response will be seen as passive and weak, rendering the potential victim more vulnerable in the face of her attacker. A definitive verbal and/or physical response which might otherwise be interpreted by someone as being rude is most appropriate. It is better to be rude than raped.
- A desire to be helpful, compassionate, involved—A common ploy that rapists use to test a potential victim is to ask for assistance: "May I use your phone? Could you show me how to get to Oak Street? Could you tell me what time it is?" Because of our religious teaching emphasizing helping those in need, loving our neighbor, etc., many of us want to respond to a request for help. However, in a rape-prone society, to respond to a request from a strange male may set us up for rape. If we are alone (at home or on the street) and a man asks for help, it may be more appropriate not to respond.

This choice not to respond is the price we all pay for the prevalence of rape in our society.

- A desire not to be "self-centered"—A concern for others but not for ourselves is a dominant theme in Christian teaching. The suggestion to respond assertively and firmly when confronted by a potential rapist may be interpreted as selfish and self-centered. Yet the Commandment to "love one another *as you love yourself*" provides a model of equal concern for both oneself and the other person. Anyone who attempts to do violence to us does not deserve our compliance. Fulfilling the love Commandment begins by loving oneself enough to stand up for oneself and refusing to be someone's doormat.

- A belief that violence is never an acceptable response to any situation—For some Christian women, non-violence is a primary value. They regard Jesus' teaching to love your enemies and turn the other cheek as mandates for a non-violent response to assault. When threatened with rape, we all face the question: "Is there a situation in which an aggressive, physical response may be necessary and appropriate to protect myself? If so, am I prepared to make such a response?" This is a question that each person, finally, must answer. Jesus' teaching was not intended to encourage us to allow ourselves to be victimized and abused. Yet the question of what specific response we are willing to make to physical attack is one that requires our prayerful consideration.

To the extent that Christian teaching prevents women from even considering self-protection seriously, it does us a disservice. We must recognize that we are vulnerable to sexual attack or abuse which is contrary to God's will for our lives. As persons created in God's own image, we are worthy of protecting ourselves from injury and abuse which contradict God's image within us.

Children in particular need to be taught how to protect themselves from a child molester. Too often children are not given the information and skills necessary to protect themselves. Furthermore, they are often taught to obey their elders without question. Children need to be taught what sexual abuse is; they should be given permission to refuse to obey an adult who would sexually exploit them. They should know that there is an adult that they can trust to help them when confronted by a child molester.[2] We spend time and energy teaching children what to do if a fire breaks out in their home or school; each year schools provide Fire Prevention Week to call attention to this problem. But little is done to teach children what to do if an adult approaches them sexually. Yet the chances that a child will be sexually molested are far greater than the chances that a child will be caught in a fire. In addition to Fire Prevention Week, we need Abuse Prevention Week in schools. Children should be taught to protect themselves.

Prevention of sexual violence requires addressing the root causes of the problem. Sexual violence is not an occasional, isolated incident experienced by individuals in an extraordinary situation. Sexual violence is a widespread problem taking place in a broad social context which allows and even encourages it to occur.[3] Rape and child sexual abuse are life-threatening by-products of a violent, sexist and racist society. Our society accepts violence as normative and inevitable. We encourage sex role differences which accentuate masculine aggression and feminine passivity. We confuse sexual activity with sexual violence to the extent of equating the two. We tend to blame the victim or blame God instead of holding the offender responsible for his acts. Until we begin to address these attitudes and practices in our society, we will not see a significant decrease in the incidence of sexual violence. The prevalence of these attitudes and practices creates a climate of tolerance of sexual violence in our society.

One major contributor to the creation of this climate of

tolerance is the media; as such, it must be examined as a root source of the problem of sexual violence. The media represents a major source of socialization and learning for most people. It is a powerful means of conveying attitudes about women, men, sexuality, and violence. In this sense, it deserves attention because of the significant role that it plays in perpetuating sexual violence. Advertising and entertainment media (including television, films, radio, print, music, etc.) provide images of women and men and how they relate to each other. Such images significantly affect our self-perceptions and behaviors. Unfortunately, the media images of women are usually negative, sexist, and consistently objectified. Women are frequently portrayed as victims of abuse. Photos of bruised and beaten women are used to sell products. Even children are made to look like sexually seductive adult women in order to catch the consumer's attention.[4] Men are portrayed as aggressive, powerful, and violent. Often images juxtapose sexuality and violence, the message being that violence inflicted on women by men is normative, harmless, and sexually exciting. In the media there are few alternative images to compete with these misrepresentations of persons.

Discussion about sexual violence and the media inevitably leads to questions about the impact of pornography.[5] Does pornography cause sexual violence or does it decrease the number of "sex" crimes by providing an outlet for offenders? To address this issue is to step into a morass of controversy that raises questions about the meaning of sexuality and the nature of pornography, its effects on human behavior, and the question of censorship.

In the past, research and discussion about pornography have arisen from two different perspectives.[6] In one, there is the assumption that sex is bad, that pornography equals sex, and therefore pornography is bad. Those who use this logic often also oppose sexuality education materials and see control of all sexually explicit materials through censorship as advisable. The opposing view assumes that sex is good, that pornography equals sex, and thus pornography is good. These people are in favor of pornography and at the same time support sexuality education and defend First Amendment rights against censorship.

Both groups equate pornography with sex. Only recently has the notion that pornography is merely sexually explicit material been called into question. Pornography is not just the portrayal of explicit sex; it is the portrayal of explicit violence or abuse in a sexual setting. A look at softcore pornography (i.e., what is available in grocery or drug stores as opposed to hardcore which is only available in adult book stores) in the past five years reveals that depictions of physical abuse, sexual violence, and children as sexual objects have increased dramatically in *Playboy, Penthouse,* and other softcore publications.[7] Images which communicate that sex is violent and violence is sexy have long been featured in hardcore pornography and they are spreading into general circulation softcore publications. The pairing of sex and violence in pornography promotes the confusion of sexual activity with sexual violence and abuse. This is a gross distortion of human sexuality which cannot help but contribute to a climate of tolerance of sexual violence.

In understanding pornography, we need to distinguish it from other forms of sexually explicit materials such as erotica, sexuality education materials, and documentary or moral realism.[8]

- *Pornography* is sexually explicit material which portrays abuse, violence, and degradation for the purpose of arousal and entertainment.
- *Erotica* describes sexual materials which may or may not be sexually explicit and are used for the purpose of arousal and entertainment. Erotica does not include any violence, abuse, or degradation of a person.
- *Sexuality education materials* are sexually explicit ma-

terials used for the purpose of education or therapy which do not include violence, abuse, or degradation.

- *Documentary* or portrayals of *moral realism* are sexually explicit and/or violent and abusive materials which depict acts of sexual abuse or violence for the purpose of documentation and critique. In these materials, the truth of the pain caused by sexual violence is accurately portrayed and the perspective taken is one of sympathy for the victims of sexual violence. The victim's humanity is always reaffirmed.

These distinctions are important if we are to understand the impact that pornography has on individuals and on society. Pornography, or explicitly violent sexual material, is becoming increasingly common and readily available. The question is what effect does it have.

Up until the mid-seventies, most of the research on pornography was based on the assumption that pornography equals sex; most of the materials studied were sexually explicit materials which did not depict violence and abuse. The conclusions most often arrived at were that such materials were harmless and, thus, that all pornography was harmless.[9] In examining pornography now, researchers are using materials which pair sex with violence and abuse. In asking what effect this material has, the research is coming up with substantially different results. Current research on pornography uses a research design (based on social learning theory) which is similar to the one used to determine that violence on television resulted in aggressive behavior in viewers. The results from the newer studies on pornography are predictable. Edward Donnerstein's research is particularly helpful. He concludes:

> . . . films which depict violence against women, even without sexual content could act as a stimulus for aggressive acts towards women. . . . There is ample evidence

that the observation of violent forms of media can facilitate aggressive responses, yet to assume that the depiction of sexual-aggression could not have a similar effect, particularly against females, would be misleading. [10]

The study conducted by Seymour Feshbach and Neal M. Malamuth provides disturbing evidence of the impact of pornography:

> College men who viewed pornography that fused sex and violence tended to be more sexually aroused by the idea of rape and less sympathetic to victims than a control group. . . . In addition, both groups of men not only identified with the rapist, but 51 percent said that they might commit rape if they were assured they would not be caught. . . . "The juxtaposition of violence with sexual excitement and satisfaction provides an unusual opportunity for conditioning of violent responses to erotic stimuli."[11]

It certainly seems reasonable that exposure to images which portray rape and sexual abuse as positive and pleasurable experiences for the victims would eventually create an impression in the observor that the aggressive exploitation of persons is normative and acceptable. In addition, the portrayal of erotic, sexually explicit images together with violent images invariably leads to the erotization of violence. When sexual violence becomes normative and violence becomes eroticized, sexual activity and sexual violence become thoroughly confused. The cultural context is set for the toleration of sexual assault and abuse.

The complex and widespread social phenomenon of pornography does appear to be one factor related to acts of sexual violence. The question then is, what do we do about it? In formulating strategies for action which address this particular root cause of sexual violence, three things are needed.

- We need to agree that pornography does present a problem to our society and that it does have a negative impact on the lives of women, men, and children. Dismissing pornography as harmless and jumping to justify its existence by protecting pornographers' First Amendment rights ignores a serious social problem in our midst.

- We need an anti-pornography strategy which is not based on government censorship. Censorship is not an effective tool to deal with pornography. Like prohibition, censorship will only drive the pornography industry further underground. And too often, censorship is used against materials other than pornography. Censorship has been used to limit erotica and sexuality education materials simply because they are sexually explicit. An anti-pornography strategy should be focused on economics. Pornography is a multimillion dollar industry because of consumers. Discouraging consumers from buying pornography will begin to limit its profitability. Zoning restrictions, advertising restrictions, pickets, and demonstrations have been successful in many communities.

- Most importantly, we need to develop a competing message. We need more sexually explicit, factual materials which portray caring, affectionate, erotic, mutually-consenting relationships between people. If the only sexually explicit materials available are violent and abusive, then people will learn from them that sexuality is degrading, exploitative, and nonconsensual. Erotica and sexuality education materials can provide a much needed alternative to pornography. Through these, the message of pornography which is, in truth, anti-sexual and anti-life will be replaced by the message of human sexual interaction which is life-giving.

Pornography is a disturbing fact of life in our society. Its presence says something very disquieting about sexuality as we know it. More and more people are becoming eroticized to violence and abuse; more and more acts of sexual violence are being committed against women, children, and men. We must face the connection that exists between these two realities. As we strategize, we must also be clear in our analysis of the problem and seek effective solutions. We must be clear that the problem with pornography is not that it is sexual but that it is violent. Concern comes not from a prudish, Victorian reaction to sexually explicit images but from a concern about the distortion of human sexuality which pornography represents and the damage that it does to our lives.

Pornography is only one aspect of our society which helps to create a climate of tolerance of sexual violence. But it is a significant aspect because it is so common and widespread. Our task must be to create a climate of intolerance of sexual violence. To do this we must tell the truth. Education is the means to truth-telling. We must tell the truth about the pain of victimization, about the responsibility that offenders carry for their actions, about the message conveyed by pornography. Every strategy for action to bring about a climate of intolerance of sexual violence begins with education. We have to know the truth about the sexual violence which pervades this society. Our survival depends on it. When we name the Unmentionable Sin, we speak the truth. And in the naming we deny its power over our lives. In naming it, the conspiracy of silence is broken. In naming it, we reclaim the truth which we know, that the way things are is not the way they have to be.

Notes

1. See Py Bateman's book, *Fear Into Anger* (Chicago: Nelson-Hall, 1978), pp. 1–123.
2. For assistance in teaching children about sexual abuse, see *He*

Told Me Not To Tell, King County Rape Relief, 1979, available at 305 S. 43rd St., Renton, Washington, 98055. See also *No More Secrets,* by Caren Adams and Jennifer Fay (San Luis Obispo, Ca.: Impact Publishers, 1981).

3. "Madison, Wis. (AP)—Amos Smith was sentenced to 14 years in prison for sexual assault yesterday despite his attorney's argument that violence against women is acceptable in American culture. His attorney, Roger Merry of Belleville, argued that Smith, 30, should not be sent to prison 'for being a victim of culture.' 'Hostility toward women, I think, is something that is culturally instilled in men,' Merry said. 'It's part of our culture that has been for hundreds of years, that violence against women is not unacceptable.'" *Seattle Times,* 1 September 1982.

4. See Jean Kilbourne's film, *Killing Us Softly,* produced by Cambridge Documentary Films, for an exposé of the images of women and children in advertising.

5. Some of this material on pornography appeared originally in "Sexual Violence," by Marie Fortune and Denise Hormann, in *JSAC Grapevine,* vol. 11, September 1979, pp. 4–5.

6. This comparison was presented in a lecture by Dr. Anne L. Ganley who drew much of her material from Irene Diamond's article, "Pornography and Repression: A Reconsideration of 'Who' and 'What,'" prepared for delivery at the Annual Meeting of the Western Social Science Association, Denver, Colorado, April 1978.

7. See Malamuth and Spinner's study reported in Laura Lederer, ed., *Take Back the Night* (New York: William Morrow and Co., 1980), p. 214.

8. These categories were originally developed by Helen Longino. These definitions represent the work of Anne L. Ganley and the author. For further discussion, see "What Is Pornography?" in Lederer, *Take Back the Night,* pp. 23–54.

9. See the President's Commission on Obscenity and Pornography (1970) as discussed by Irene Diamond in Lederer, *Take Back the Night,* p. 192.

10. Edward Donnerstein as quoted in Lederer, *Take Back the Night,* p. 230.

11. Seymour Feshbach and Neal M. Malamuth as reported in Lederer, *Take Back the Night,* pp. 215–16.

239

Excerpts from *I Choose to Remember* are used by permission of the Violet Collective, Minneapolis, Minnesota. Material is from a tape, distributed by Chec, Inc., St. Paul, Minnesota.

Excerpts from *Rape: The Price of Coercive Sexuality* by Lorenne Clark and Debra Lewis are reprinted by permission of The Women's Press, Toronto. Copyright © 1977 Lorenne M.G. Clark and Debra J. Lewis.